To
Haddon Robinson
Teacher, Mentor and Master Communicator

STOP PREACHING AND START COMMUNICATING

COMMUNICATION PRINCIPLES PREACHERS CAN LEARN FROM TELEVISION

TONY GENTILUCCI

Foreword by Haddon Robinson

CASTLE QUAY BOOKS

STOP PREACHING AND START COMMUNICATING
Copyright ©2010 Tony Gentilucci
All rights reserved
Printed in Canada
International Standard Book Number: 978-1-894860-48-2

Published by:
Castle Quay Books
1307 Wharf Street, Pickering, Ontario, L1W 1A5
Tel: (416) 573-3249   Fax: (416) 291-8003
E-mail: info@castlequaybooks.com
www.castlequaybooks.com

Copy editing by Lori Mackay, Janet Dimond and Marina Hofman
Cover design by Alain Demers of Vision Design Studio
All diagrams, graphs and charts designed by Agripino Monteiro of Ace Graphic Design
Storyboard design by Mark Simon of Animatics & Storyboards, Inc.
Printed at Essence Publishing, Belleville, Ontario

This book or parts thereof may not be reproduced in any form without prior written permission of the publishers.

Library and Archives Canada Cataloguing in Publication

Gentilucci, Tony, 1966-

  Stop preaching and start communicating: communication principles preachers can learn from television / Tony Gentilucci.

Includes bibliographical references and index.
ISBN 978-1-894860-48-2

         1. Preaching. 2. Mass media--Religious aspects--Christianity. I. Title.
BV4211.3.G45 2010   251   C2010-901994-6

All Scripture quotations, unless otherwise specified, are from *The Holy Bible, King James Version.* Copyright © 1977, 1984, Thomas Nelson Inc., Publishers. • Scripture quotations marked NLT are taken from *The Holy Bible,* New Living Translation. Copyright © 1996. Used by permission of Tyndale House Publishers, Inc., Wheaton, IL 60187. All rights reserved. • Scripture marked NIV are taken from the HOLY BIBLE, NEW INTERNATIONAL VERSION ®. Copyright © 1973, 1978, 1984 by International Bible Society. Used by permission of Zondervan Publishing House. All rights reserved.

*"The day of the preacher is over;
the day of the communicator is here."*

—Haddon Robinson—

Contents

Acknowledgements 9
Foreword 11
Introduction 13

PART I
THE FACTS ABOUT TELEVISION

ONE	*In the Beginning*	19
TWO	*Just the Facts*	31

PART II
COMMUNICATION PRINCIPLES PREACHERS CAN LEARN FROM TELEVISION

THREE	*Who Are You Talking To?*	51
FOUR	*On the Air*	65
FIVE	*Let's Talk*	89
SIX	*Teleprompting the Text*	109
SEVEN	*What's the Point?*	129
EIGHT	*Tricks of the Trade*	149
NINE	*Call Now!*	169
TEN	*Until Next Time*	191

Conclusion 203
Appendix—Answers to Exercise in Chapter 7 209
Bibliography 211

Acknowledgements

It takes more than just one person to complete a significant endeavor. And if anyone tells you otherwise watch for their nose to grow! I'd like to take this opportunity to acknowledge some of the wonderful people who helped me with this project.

To begin, I would like to thank Haddon Robinson. Sir, it was an absolute honor and a privilege to sit under you. Thank you for all of the valuable direction you gave me during this project and I hope I'm as cool and as hip as you are when I get to your age. You so get it Sir! I love you.

To Sid Buzzell I say, thank you for sending me back to the drawing board more than once. You and Haddon both taught me that good writing is in the rewriting and that less, truly is more. Sid, thank you for pushing me to not settle for anything less, and your encouragement throughout the project was much appreciated. I want to thank Andy Stanley, who I believe is one of the most gifted communicators I know. Andy, thank you for your time and your support. You rock, my friend!

I want to thank Alain Demers who was so patient and cooperative with me as we worked together in designing the cover of the book. You nailed it, Alain! It was a pleasure to work with you. To my good and long-time friend Agripino Monteiro who is truly one of the most talented graphic artists I have the pleasure of working with. You did an outstanding job in designing all of the diagrams, graphs and charts throughout the book. It's a delight to know you Agripino. Thank you to Mark Simon and Jeanne Pappas Simon who did an excellent job on the design and script of the storyboard.

Thank you to Lori Mackay, Janet Dimond and Marina Hofman, the three ladies who helped me with the editing and proofreading of this project. Your dedication and attention to detail was second to none. And thank you to Cindy Thompson for superbly managing all of the details of the printing process from beginning to end. Cindy, you are so good at what you do! To my good friend Larry Willard of Castle Quay Books, what can I say other than thank you, thank you, and again thank you for taking this project on and for believing in it. Your personal drive and motivation to never give up are an inspiration to me, Larry.

I also want to thank my sister Liliana, who was my cheerleader as she read through the manuscript. Thanks for all your positive feedback Lil. And thank you to my wife Lidia, who was always there to discuss ideas with me, whether it was at 6:00 in the morning or 11:00 at night.

Foreword
by Haddon Robinson

There are times when I wish my students had never heard of "preaching a sermon." When many of them think of "preaching," they picture someone in a robe talking in a stained-glass tone of voice saying things that matter as though they don't. Others see an overweight man gasping for breath hollering at people as though they were deaf. Inhabitants of the 21st century don't trust preachers and don't like sermons. Sermons use a strange vocabulary that only the initiated who know the code can understand. Preachers ask questions no one ever asks or solve problems that have never arisen and then provide answers relatively few listeners take seriously.

Is this a caricature? Of course it is. But it is not far off from the picture people in the pew or people on the pavement have of those of us who deliver sermons. In their minds, the hour from eleven to twelve on Sunday morning ranks as the most boring hour of the week. Jesus Christ is the most fascinating person in the universe, but somehow the way he is introduced each week betrays his greatness.

Perhaps we preachers might get more across if instead of preaching a sermon we thought of ourselves as communicating a message. If we approached our task with that assignment, we might consider that no method is out of bounds that contributes to our purpose to make Christ known. As Paul, God's special messenger, declared in his Corinthian correspondence, he will do anything short of sinning to communicate the gospel.

Isn't it a bit short-sighted to conclude that we can learn nothing from the men and women in the media who will do anything, including sinning, to move the merchandise? Even though we may question both their message and some of their methods, we can "spoil the Egyptians," aware that if we eat at their table we are wise to use a long spoon.

We must not sacrifice the message of the Bible to gain a hearing. What good is it to be more effective if in the process we have nothing significant to say to those who stop to listen? Content always trumps method, yet new methods or different methods can make old truth appealing.

If you are open to learning from secular theorists, then read this book. Tony knows the world of media and the word of Christ. He brings the two together so that even as we continue to preach God's word we may do so more effectively.

Haddon W. Robinson, Ph.D.
Harold John Ockenga Distinguished Professor of Preaching
Gordon-Conwell Theological Seminary

Introduction

The first week of my first Doctorate of Ministry residency at Gordon-Conwell Theological Seminary in Boston was co-taught by Duane Litfin and Haddon Robinson, two extraordinary communicators. During one of Duane's lectures, everything in me stopped. I sat motionless as I heard him quote this line from Haddon Robinson: "The day of the preacher is over; the day of the communicator is here." That one sentence had such a tremendous impact on me that I couldn't write it down fast enough. And for the rest of the day I found myself thinking about that one line over and over again because of the effect it had on me. I completely agree with Haddon. The day of the preacher is over and the day of the communicator is here.

Haddon later clarified for me the difference between a preacher and a communicator:

> When I make that comparison, it's not a put-down. There are people who preach within their tradition, and they do very well. I think the communicator is somebody who is aware of the wider audience and the wider culture, and so therefore he doesn't really think of himself as preaching a message as much as communicating a message. And so it's an attitude as well as a style. And I think that communicators are the ones that are needed today to bridge the gap to a secular society.[1]

---

[1] Personal interview with Haddon Robinson, 2 September 2005.

I like what Robert Duffet said about this in his book *A Relevant Word*: "I prefer to use the term *communicating* rather than *preaching* the gospel. The result is a message rather than a sermon."[2]

Rick Warren explains: "Our English word for communication comes from the Latin word *communis*, which means 'common.' And you can't communicate with people until you find something you have in common with them."[3]

I think you would agree that most unchurched people believe that preachers don't have anything in common with them. Mention the word *preacher* to your unchurched colleagues, friends and family members, and they may quickly respond with words like Bible thumper, loud, arrogant, judgmental, condescending, narrow-minded and know-it-all. So how do we bridge the gap between our secular society and the communication of God's Word? I believe the answer to that question is wrapped up in one word: television.

You may be thinking, *Television? What on earth can that evil one-eyed monster teach me about communicating God's Word effectively?* You will find the answer as you read this book. When Jesus communicated to the people of His day, He did it in the language of the day. He spoke in a manner that they understood. He talked about birds and seeds and farmers and fields. He knew His world, and His world knew Him. He didn't remain distant and detached from the world. He entered it. He rolled up His sleeves and pushed His way in. He touched the world, and the world touched Him.

Today, television is the communications medium that people turn to more than any other to stay in touch with what's going on in the world. Statistics tell us that the average person watches almost five hours of television a day. It is by far the most effective, persuasive and influential communications medium of our day. It truly does have an enormous impact on our culture. Having spent my working life in the

---

[2] Robert Duffet, *A Relevant Word: Communicating the Gospel to Seekers* (Valley Forge, PA: Judson Press, 1995), xv.
[3] Rick Warren, "Preaching to the Unchurched," *Preaching* 12, no. 2 (September-October 1996): 4.

world of radio and television, I can say that the people behind the medium of television must be doing something right.

This book examines television as a communications medium, its presentation methods and its delivery techniques, to consider what we, as oral communicators of the most important message the world needs to hear, can learn from it. My prayer is that as you read this book you will become more aware of what television does effectively so that you can incorporate some of its principles into your own communication style. You may even be challenged to rethink the three-points-and-a-poem outline, the predictable alliterations and the cute acrostics, and instead begin to communicate with people in common everyday language.

In short, my prayer is that you'll stop preaching and start communicating.

Part One

THE FACTS ABOUT TELEVISION

1

IN THE BEGINNING

"I know that God exists. I know that I have never invented anything. I have been a medium by which these things were given to the culture as fast as the culture could earn them. I give all the credit to God."

—Philo Taylor Farnsworth—

In the beginning was the word—the spoken word, that is. At the dawn of time, the first and only mode of communication was oral. In fact, before any other form of communication existed in any given society, oral communication was the primary means of conveying one's ideals, ideas and values from one generation to the next. The father told the son, the son told the grandson, the grandson told the great-grandson. It was all transmitted by word of mouth. As communication progressed, picture communication developed, with symbols used to represent objects, activities, places, events and eventually ideas.[4] The

---

[4] Cave paintings were the first form of picture communication. Then came petroglyphs, which involved carving into a rock surface. Petroglyphs evolved into pictograms. While petroglyphs would simply show an event, pictograms would tell a story about the event. Finally, pictograms evolved into ideograms, graphical symbols that represented ideas. Pictograms could represent only something resembling their form; for example, a circle could represent a sun but not concepts like heat, light or day. Ideograms, however, could convey more abstract concepts.

invention of television was thousands of years in the future, but we see the seed in the way people communicated.

As picture communication evolved, it slowly lost its detail and became abstract figures representing sounds in spoken communication, which brought about the alphabet and writing and later the introduction of paper.

A Communication Revolution

In AD 1436, an invention was created that literally caused a communication revolution and was the springboard for many other modes of communication we know today. It was invented by a hardworking German tradesman born over 600 years ago. He wasn't a brilliant philosopher or theorist. He wasn't even a good businessman. But he was persistent and clever, working for years to perfect one invention. His invention? The printing press. His name? Johannes Gutenberg.

Gutenberg's breakthrough came when he combined earlier printing techniques introduced by the Chinese and Koreans with a new design for moveable metal type. And then he put it all together with a press similar to one used to make olive oil. With this, printing history was made.[5]

In 1999, A&E examined the lives of 100 people over the previous 1,000 years and chose Gutenberg as the number one person of the millennium. Walter Isaacson, former managing editor of *Time* magazine, said:

> Gutenberg would be surprised I think to be number one, because he was not a genius. Newton knew he was a genius. Copernicus knew he was changing the whole way we looked at the world. But Gutenberg was sort of the tinkerer, the shopkeeper, somebody who puts something together. And yet, the invention of the printing press, even if it isn't the great genius who did it, transformed our society perhaps as much as the theory of gravity or the theory of calculus.[6]

---

[5] *Biography of the Millennium*, Harry Smith, host and narrator, A&E, 1999.
[6] Walter Isaacson, *Biography of the Millennium*, Harry Smith, host and narrator, A&E, 1999.

GETTING THE WORD OUT

When Gutenberg printed 200 copies of the Holy Bible in 1455, it marked a turning point in our civilization. Previously, almost the only time anyone heard anything about the outside world was when someone arrived with news. And with the invention of printing and the publishing of books there was for the first time a generation gap. A son no longer had to depend on his father for wisdom and values because he could learn from the wisdom of others by reading books. Before Gutenberg's invention, one of the major canons of education was memorization. With the coming of books, the emphasis on memory declined. Books allowed education to become linear—line upon line—which made it easier to deal with an abstract concept, because you could read about it and then read it again.

Gutenberg continued in the printing trade until his death in 1468, but he was always short of money. In fact, when his splendid Bible appeared, all of his profits went to his creditors. Yet, what he created was astonishing. Within 50 years, 20 million books had been printed in Europe. And in another 100 years that number increased tenfold.[7] Isaacson explained:

> We evolve from being a society that was all city-states and villages that didn't communicate to being a global society in which all information can be communicated, and it starts with the printing press.[8]

THOUGHTS BLOSSOM

Gutenberg's breakthrough helped Renaissance thought to blossom and spread and Martin Luther's Protestant Reformation to attract new followers. Then came the scientific discoveries of Descartes, Galileo and Newton and of course the Industrial Revolution. News of technological breakthroughs, innovations, politics and the arts all spread quickly through newspapers, pamphlets and journals.

---

[7] *Biography of the Millennium.*
[8] Isaacson, *Biography of the Millennium.*

Gutenberg's printing press unleashed the power of ideas, and in many ways his information revolution was just the beginning. Isaacson confirmed:

> Gutenberg allowed us to transmit information so much more easily and freely. And that continues through to the current day with the invention of radio at the beginning of the century, then of television, then of the Internet and e-mail. It begins with Gutenberg, and it's a 500-year process.[9]

No Gutenberg, No…

Virtually everyone who has made any kind of impact in the world, whether good or bad, owes a debt to Johannes Gutenberg. Consider those who wrote and published their theories and ideas like Darwin and his *Origin of Species*, Jefferson's Declaration of Independence and even Hitler's *Mein Kampf*. Were it not for Gutenberg, they might not have been inspired to greatness or infamy by reading the works of others. And their own thoughts and ideas would not have survived beyond their own lifetimes to influence future generations.[10]

As well, the creations and discoveries of artists like Michelangelo and Picasso, Beethoven and the Beatles and scientists like Marie Curie, Alexander Fleming and Sigmund Freud have been reproduced on the printed page or broadcast on radio and television and are now available to whole new audiences via the Internet, thanks again to the printer from Mainz, Germany.[11]

The Little Black Box

At the beginning of the 1900s, 500 years after Gutenberg's invention of the printing press, came another invention that would dramatically change the face of communication. The introduction of electronics would supercharge the powers of mass media. Now communication could be not only read but heard.

---

[9] Ibid.
[10] *Biography of the Millennium.*
[11] Ibid.

Stop Preaching and Start Communicating

When Guglielmo Marconi was en route to Britain at the turn of the century, he was stopped at customs because officials there thought that his black boxes were bombs and had them destroyed. The devices young Marconi was carrying were explosive, but not in the way the officers imagined. They were another invention that would change the way the world communicates—radio.[12] Marconi's radio enabled a message to reach millions of ears in an instant, and for a brief time it was the most advanced means of mass communication.

MARCONI—HERO OF THE TITANIC DISASTER

At the age of 21, Marconi figured out how to send a message through the air without wires, and within a short time he was transmitting all the way across the Atlantic. In essence, the invention of radio removed the restraints of wires and connections. A perfect example of this was the *Titanic* disaster. When the huge ship began to sink in the early hours of April 15, 1912, the shocking news was relayed across the Atlantic by Marconi operators. Tragically, the message from the liner *Virginian* to the *Californian*, the ship nearest the *Titanic* when it went down, was to no avail. It was sent at 4 a.m., nearly 2 hours after the *Titanic* sank, but was not picked up by the *Californian*'s lone wireless operator, because he was asleep. Despite these sad facts, Marconi was acknowledged as the hero of the *Titanic* disaster, because without his radio on board and the wireless distress signals that were sent out, the fate of the ship would have remained a mystery and no one would have survived.[13]

RADIO GOES SATELLITE

Today, the United States has over 13,800 radio stations, more than any other country in the world. Of that number, 4,854 are AM sta-

---

[12] Ibid.
[13] Gavin Weightman, *Signor Marconi's Magic Box: The Most Remarkable Invention of the 19th Century and the Amateur Inventor Whose Genius Sparked a Revolution* (Cambridge, MA: Da Capo Press), 2003, 222ff in the photo section.

tions, while 8,950 are FM stations.[14] But by far the most revolutionary change that the radio industry has experienced since Marconi sent out that first radio signal was the introduction of satellite radio.

Satellite radio is more than the latest technology. It's an extraordinary way to experience your favorite music, sports, news, talk and comedy programs. And wherever you go, it goes. No longer are your choices limited to local stations. Satellite radio gives you the freedom to hear what you want, when you want. Imagine dozens and dozens of uninterrupted commercial-free music channels playing all of your new and old favorites. You can choose from pop, rock, dance, jazz, country, Christian and classical. Then under each category there are subcategories. For example, under pop you can choose from light pop, love songs, easy listening and top 40 hits. Under rock, you can select early classic rock, pure hard rock, classic hard rock or heavy metal. If you like country, there are today's country hits, classic country and bluegrass. The variety is truly amazing. In addition, there are sports channels that carry all of the latest scores, sports news and heart-pounding coverage of your favorite pro and college teams; national news broadcasts from sources like CNN, MSNBC, Fox News and BBC; and talk shows you rely on to inform and provoke you. It even includes traffic and weather from every major U.S. city, whether it's Detroit, Dallas, New York or L.A. That's satellite radio. Not to mention the thousands of radio stations available worldwide via the Internet with just a few simple strokes on a keyboard. We've sure come a long way since 1894, when Guglielmo Marconi was just 20 years old. At that time, there was no such thing as wireless, and radio was just a dream in a young man's mind.

THE BIRTH OF SIGHT AND SOUND

While Marconi's radio was transforming the face of communication in the early 1900s, there was something even greater being worked

---

[14] Central Intelligence Agency, "Field Listing—Radio Broadcast Stations," *The World Factbook*, <https://www.cia.gov/library/publications/the-world-factbook/fields/2013.html>, accessed 13 December 2007.

on that would unite audio and video. In fact, the early years of radio seem to have been only a transition into the age of what has been called the ultimate mass communications medium—television.

American engineer Philo Farnsworth was born on August 19, 1906, on Indian Creek in Beaver County, Utah. His parents expected him to become a concert violinist, but his interests drew him to experiments with electricity. At the age of 12, he built an electric motor and produced the first electric washing machine his family had ever owned.

Philo Farnsworth attended Brigham Young University in Utah, where he researched television picture transmission. While in high school, Philo Farnsworth had already conceived of his ideas for television. In 1926, he co-founded Crocker Research Laboratories, which he later renamed Farnsworth Television, Inc. in 1929....

In 1927, Philo Farnsworth was the first inventor to transmit a television image, comprised of 60 horizontal lines. The image transmitted was a dollar sign. Farnsworth developed the dissector tube, the basis of all current electronic televisions. He filed for his first television patent in 1927.[15]

THE NEW YORK WORLD'S FAIR

In 1928, the Federal Radio Commission issued the first television license, and in 1930, the first television commercial was aired. By 1936, there were about 200 television sets in use worldwide. And, in 1939, television was demonstrated at the New York World's Fair.

Haddon Robinson was just nine years old when he attended the World's Fair that year, and he clearly remembers the television demonstration that he witnessed:

> It was 1939, and I was just a kid. I remember going to the World's Fair. It was a fair that promised everything. The alabaster cities would finally gleam. There would be no crime. And everything would be a marvelous world of technology.

---

[15] Mary Bellis, "Inventors: Philo Farnsworth," <http://www.inventors.about.com/library/inventors/blfarnsworth.htm>, accessed 24 September 2005.

They were wrong about most of it, but they were right about television. I remember going into a room and you can stand in front of this camera and people in the next room can see you. When I was a kid, I grew up in a home in which our folks, part of a fairly tight religious system, felt movies were wrong. But at the World's Fair they promised that there would come a day where we would have television in every home. It was almost too much for a kid to believe. The first ride in a car I got at the New York World's Fair. The Ford Company was there promoting their cars…the first ride I ever got, at nine years of age. I could believe that there could be cars in the future, but to have movies in your home? I heard so many arguments about supporting Hollywood and all that stuff, but it was amazing how fast it happened.

In the 1940s they [televisions] got into all the bars in New York and into some of the homes. People would buy a television set, which was postage-stamp size, and people all over the neighborhood would come over and watch the television with you. The ball games would be televised in New York. When I was a kid, I worked as a messenger, and I would go from bar to bar, or I should say, from the door of one bar to the door of another bar, [*Laughter*] and I would watch an inning, then they would go to commercials and I would leave. And then in the '50s they got into the homes. And by the end of the '50s, the continent was tied together. And radio went to being background music. And television became the dominant medium in our culture.[16]

King of all Media

There is no doubt that much has changed in the way we communicate from the time those first editions of the Holy Bible rolled off the printing press several hundred years ago. And there is also no

---

[16] Haddon Robinson, "Preaching in a Television Age," *TV and Story*, Preaching Today, cassette no. 145.

doubt that it was Gutenberg's printing press that started it all. Yet, television is not just a passing phenomenon, despite even the introduction of the Internet, which is nothing more than an extension of television on computer. In fact, for more than five decades, television has been the sun around which all other media forms orbit. Television's impact on American society and the world is the greatest in our history.

> Television is omnipresent. And we have now moved in our society to a postliterate society. The way in which people get ideas, the way in which they shape their ideals, comes not because they read books but because they see it. They visualize it. It's on television.... In the world out there, people are oriented to images. We are in a postliterate age. Twenty-seven million Americans are functionally illiterate. They can't read the print on a cereal box. Another group equally as large can read only in the widest definition of the term, but give them a paragraph and they cannot tell you what that paragraph is about. Eighty million Americans are operationally illiterate. They read a newspaper, they read the headlines, they read the comics, they read a paragraph of the sports pages. Generally speaking, people do not get their news today from news magazines and newspapers. Well over half of our population says when they get their news they get it by watching television.... That means a great deal to people involved in communication. It means that if you believe the way you're going to communicate your message to men and women today is by putting it into print, you don't understand the culture out there. And that has shaped the way we think. We see things in images. We visualize things. It affects the way we preach. It affects the hard core of communication. And I believe the thing that shapes our values most in our society is television.[17]

---

[17] Haddon Robinson, "Our Mission in a Changing World," Denver Seminary, 4 January 1991.

Think of it: television reaches everywhere. Today, there is no place it cannot or does not go. Its cameras literally roam the world, and its receiver sets are as common as refrigerators, stoves and telephones. In every way imaginable, the invention of the television has truly transformed the history of communication. Watching television is a lot like being there. In fact, it's the mother ship of virtual reality, separating viewers from the action or event by nothing more than a transparent screen. Television takes its viewers across time and space to witness an enormous variety of experiences that they couldn't possibly live through in more than 100 lifetimes. Viewers can love, learn, laugh and cry as they watch a wide array of lives lived out on the screen. They can see how the world looked 1,000 years ago, and they can see how it may look 1,000 years from now. In short, viewers have as many eyes as they have television channels. And today, with digital cable and satellite TV at our fingertips, the number of channels is in the hundreds.

And if that weren't enough, today there's even television-to-go. No more VCRs, no more tapes. You can now watch your favorite programs from anywhere in the world. There are several devices that allow you to take your TV programs on the road with you and watch them at your leisure, whether you're sitting in a coffee shop or riding in a taxi. Technology goes even farther and allows you to watch TV programs from anywhere with an Internet connection.[18] And if you think that's amazing, it gets even better—you can now watch television on your cell phone. For years, people selling other types of media advertising, like radio or print, would discourage their clients from buying television because it wasn't portable. You couldn't take it with you. That's no longer the case, with many cell phone companies offering mobile TV. Now you can watch a variety of channels anywhere, anytime. You can get the latest sports, breaking news and up-to-the-minute weather reports around the clock, 24/7. These latest developments clearly show that there are no signs that television will die. Instead, the medium continues to evolve and flourish.

In short, there is no doubt that television is the most influential and dominant medium among all of the communications media available today.

Stop Preaching and Start Communicating

[18] There are several ways you can take your favorite TV programs on the road with you. [1] Record them on a data card. The V-Mate from ScanDisk is a wallet-sized box that plugs into a video source such as your cable box or DVD player. It records video on a removable data card, such as an SD card or Sony Memory Stick, and can squeeze up to 3.5 hours of programming on a single one-GB data card, giving you plenty of space for multiple episodes. [2] Record them to DVD. You can then take the DVDs with you and play them back on your laptop or any DVD player attached to a TV. [3] Record them on a laptop loaded with Windows 7, an operating system from Microsoft that includes a built-in program called Windows Media Center, which can record TV shows when connected to a cable or satellite box. [4] Finally, use the Slingbox gadget from the California company Sling Media. You connect the Slingbox to your digital cable box and to your high-speed Internet service, then load the Slingbox software onto your laptop. On the road, you connect your laptop to a high-speed Internet connection and call up the Slingbox software. The Slingbox back home pushes the television signal from your living room across the Internet to your laptop screen, so you are, in effect, watching your home TV on your computer screen. Also, on-screen is a virtual remote control so you can channel hop just as easily as if you were sprawled on your living room couch. Sling Media also has the SlingCatcher. Once connected to the Internet, this little box receives the signal from your Slingbox back home and pipes it onto any screen, including your hotel room television.

2

JUST THE FACTS

"If we do not get with the modern communications program, people will turn us off in a heartbeat. A generation accustomed to the swift-moving images and infinite choices of satellite and cable television, as well as the lifelikeness of video technology, will not tolerate a boring, lifeless, drab presentation of the gospel."

—Jerry Vines—

This chapter is designed to do exactly what the title says—give you "just the facts" about the impact and influence that television has on our society. A picture is truly worth a thousand words, so the material is presented in graph and tabular form.

PENETRATION TOPS 98%

In 1950, only 9% of U.S. households had a television set. Within 5 years it shot up to almost 65%, and by 1965 it reached over 92%. From there it has grown to its current level of just under 99%, meaning that almost every household in America has a television set.

Nearly Every Household Has a Television

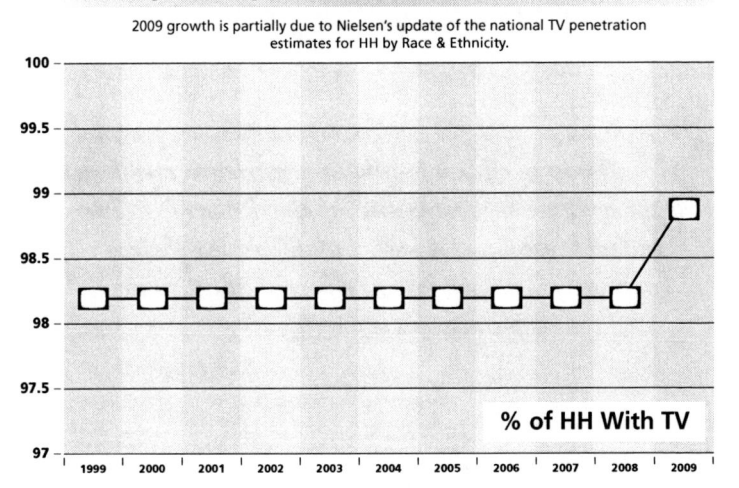

2009 growth is partially due to Nielsen's update of the national TV penetration estimates for HH by Race & Ethnicity.

% of HH With TV

Television Bureau of Advertising 2009 TV Basis and The Nielsen Company

More Than One Per Household

Households with 2 or more sets accounted for only 1% of the total in 1950. That number grew to over 50% by 1980 and is now over 82%. Color TVs in households started later, but penetration increased faster. By 1980, it had reached 83%, and today it has reached complete saturation at 99.9%.

Multi-Set Households are Common

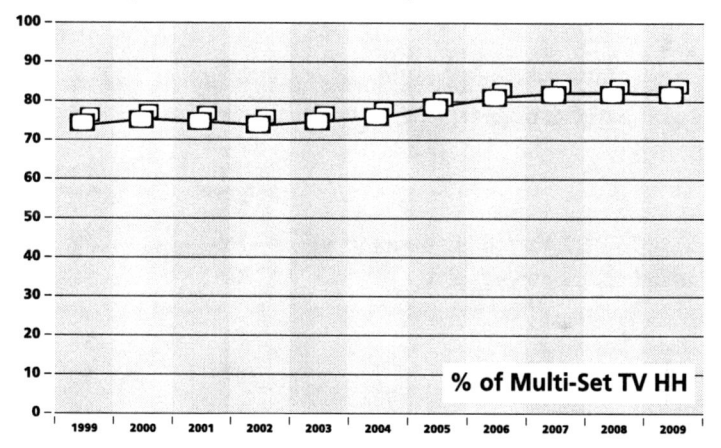

In 2006, the 80% mark was crossed, and it rose to 82.1% in 2009

% of Multi-Set TV HH

Television Bureau of Advertising 2009 TV Basis and The Nielsen Company

In Every Room of the House

When television first entered the home, the whole family would gather around to watch a single TV set in the living room. As we all know, those days are long gone. Today, sets are likely to be in not only the living room but also the family room, bedroom and even the kitchen. This means that advertisers now have an even greater opportunity to target the right audience at the right time. The following table shows that 74% of TV households have a set in the living room, followed closely by 61% with a set in the master bedroom.

**Viewing Doesn't Just Occur in the Living Room
TV Sets are Used in Every Room of the House**

	% TV HH with sets in the...	% of total household TV sets
Living/front/sitting room, parlor	74	27
Family/rec./play room, den	34	14
Study, library, office, computer	7	3
Master bedroom	61	22
Child's bedroom	21	10
Other bedroom	23	10
Kitchen	16	6
Dining room	2	1
Basement	7	3
Garage, porch, workshop, attic	4	2
Other	5	4

Television Bureau of Advertising 2009 TV Basis and Knowledge Networks/SRI, The Home Technology Monitor 2008 Ownership & Trend Report (excludes Alaska & Hawaii)

HOUSEHOLD VIEWING TOPS 8 HOURS A DAY

In the 1950s, TV households averaged between 4.5 and 5 hours of TV viewing a day. By the '60s it reached 5 to 6 hours. In the '70s and '80s, with multi-set and color households growing and stations extending the broadcast day, viewing increased to more than 6 hours daily. In the '90s, with a wide selection of 24-hour programming, households were averaging over 7 hours a day. Viewing increased to more than 8 hours a day in 2004 and has climbed steadily ever since.

Household Viewing Tops 8 Hours

As Options Have Expanded, So Has the Amount of Time Households Devote to Television

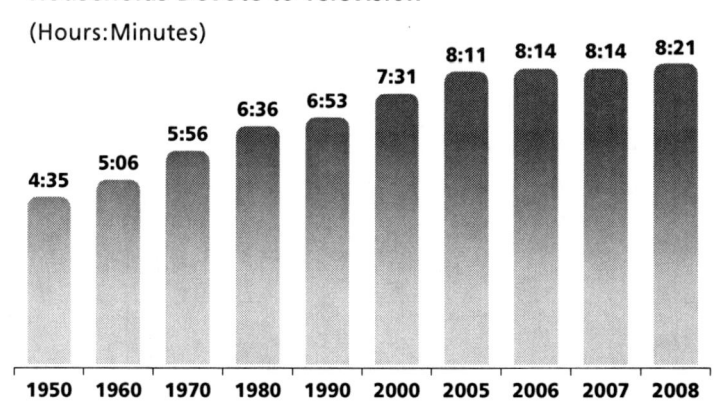

(Hours:Minutes)

Year	Hours:Minutes
1950	4:35
1960	5:06
1970	5:56
1980	6:36
1990	6:53
2000	7:31
2005	8:11
2006	8:14
2007	8:14
2008	8:21

Television Bureau of Advertising 2009 TV Basis and The Nielsen Company, NTI Annual Averages Prior to 9/87: Audimeter Sample; 9/87 to date: People Meter Sample

WOMEN WATCH MORE

Traditionally, women in TV households have spent the most time viewing television, averaging almost 5.5 hours a day. Men are next, coming very close to the 5 hour mark. Teens and children have been viewing at about equal levels, totaling almost 3.5 hours each per day. In 2008, all segments posted gains. Women were still number one with up to 5 hours 25 minutes. Men increased their viewing by 10 minutes and came in at 4 hours 49 minutes, while teens increased by 3 minutes to 3 hours 27 minutes, and children increased by one minute to 3 hours 28 minutes.

While Women View More Television, All Family Members Tune In

(Time Spent Per Day)

	Men	Women	Teens	Children
2002	4:22	4:58	3:09	3:10
2003	4:29	5:05	3:07	3:14
2004	4:26	5:07	3:07	3:16
2005	4:31	5:17	3:19	3:19
2006	4:35	5:17	3:22	3:26
2007	4:39	5:19	3:24	3:27
2008	4:49	5:25	3:27	3:28

Television Bureau of Advertising 2009 TV Basis and The Nielsen Company, NTI Annual Averages

Top Choice for Entertainment

The following graph shows how many hours per year a person spends watching television. It's clear that no other medium comes close.

Television is the Top Choice for Entertainment

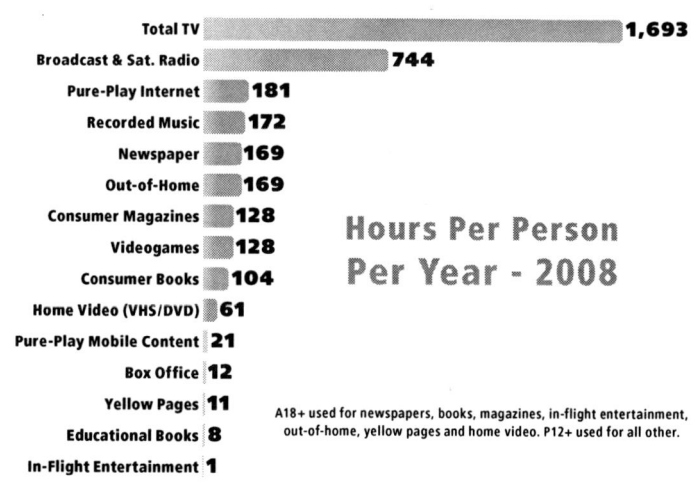

Hours Per Person Per Year - 2008

Total TV	1,693
Broadcast & Sat. Radio	744
Pure-Play Internet	181
Recorded Music	172
Newspaper	169
Out-of-Home	169
Consumer Magazines	128
Videogames	128
Consumer Books	104
Home Video (VHS/DVD)	61
Pure-Play Mobile Content	21
Box Office	12
Yellow Pages	11
Educational Books	8
In-Flight Entertainment	1

A18+ used for newspapers, books, magazines, in-flight entertainment, out-of-home, yellow pages and home video. P12+ used for all other.

Television Bureau of Advertising 2009 TV Basis and Veronis Suhler Stevenson Communications Industry Forescast 2009 – 2013

MORE TIME DAILY

In the average day, adults 18 and older spend more time with television than with newspapers, radio, magazines and the Internet combined. Similar dominance is seen across all demographic groups.

Adults Spend More Time with Television Each Day Than They Do with Any Other Medium

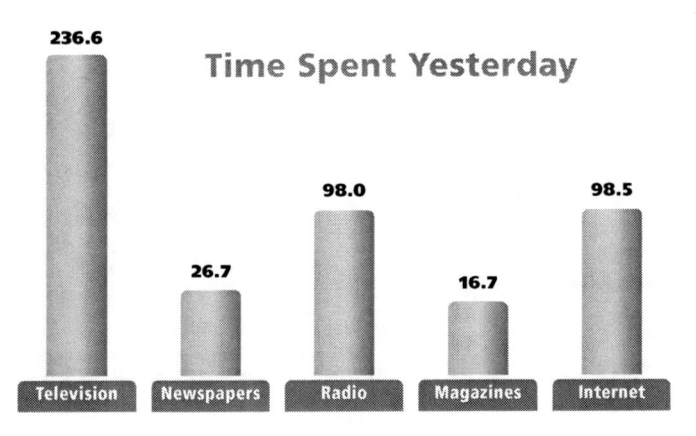

Time Spent Yesterday

- Television: 236.6
- Newspapers: 26.7
- Radio: 98.0
- Magazines: 16.7
- Internet: 98.5

Television Bureau of Advertising 2009 TV Basis and TVB, Nielsen Media Research Custom Survey 2008

REACHES MORE ADULTS PER DAY

Television reaches over 90% of adults 18 and older in the average day, while radio reaches just over 73% and the Internet over 65%. The same holds true across all demographic groups.

Television Reaches More Adults Each Day than Any Other Medium

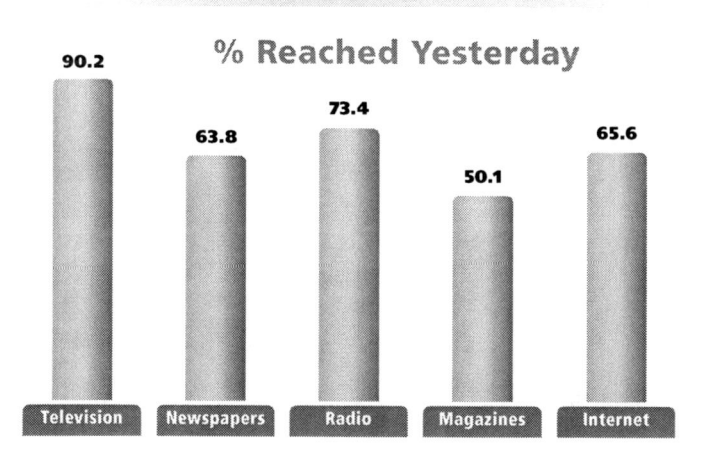

% Reached Yesterday

Television	Newspapers	Radio	Magazines	Internet
90.2	63.8	73.4	50.1	65.6

Television Bureau of Advertising 2009 TV Basis and TVB, Nielsen Media Research Custom Survey 2008

Advertisers Spend More

Newspapers had been the number one ad medium in the U.S. since 1776. In 1994, the advertising community, voting with their dollars, made TV number one for the first time. Since then, TV has widened its lead over newspapers by almost $30 billion.

Advertisers Spend More Money on Television

Television Surpassed Newspapers in 1994, and has held the lead ever since.

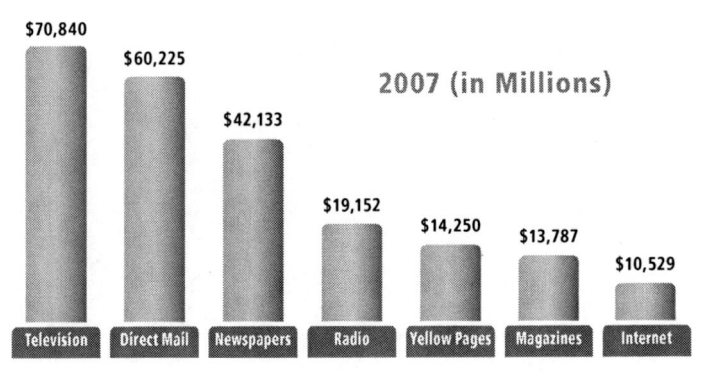

2007 (in Millions)

- Television: $70,840
- Direct Mail: $60,225
- Newspapers: $42,133
- Radio: $19,152
- Yellow Pages: $14,250
- Magazines: $13,787
- Internet: $10,529

Television Bureau of Advertising 2009 TV Basis and Universal McCann (1)

Most Authoritative and Exciting Advertising

The public's perception of advertising in media is critical to the process of selling products and services. Television gets half the votes for *most authoritative* and close to 80% for *most exciting*. This is driven by TV's ability to deliver the advertiser's message using sight, sound, motion, emotion and color.

Television Advertising Has the Best Perception Among Adults

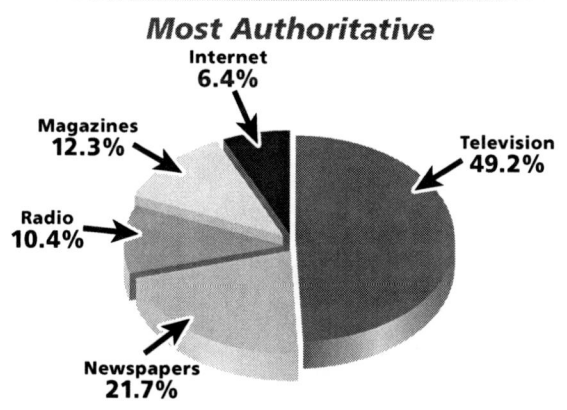

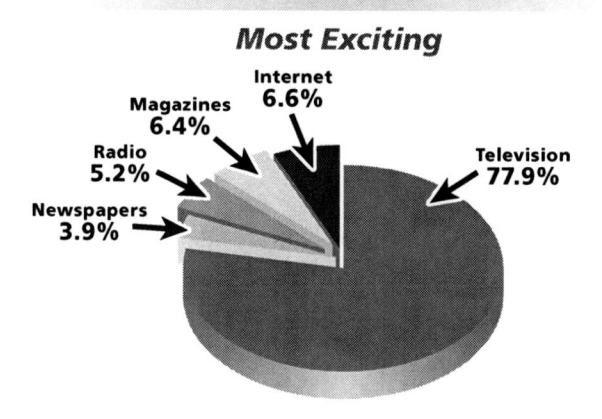

Most Authoritative

- Television 49.2%
- Newspapers 21.7%
- Magazines 12.3%
- Radio 10.4%
- Internet 6.4%

Television Bureau of Advertising 2009 TV Basis and TVB, Nielsen Media Research Custom Survey 2008

Television Advertising Has the Best Perception Among Adults

Most Exciting

- Television 77.9%
- Internet 6.6%
- Magazines 6.4%
- Radio 5.2%
- Newspapers 3.9%

Television Bureau of Advertising 2009 TV Basis and TVB, Nielsen Media Research Custom Survey 2008

Most Influential and Persuasive Advertising

Advertising agencies like using a medium that is both influential and persuasive. They like the idea that television has the power to induce belief and action in people. For this reason TV wins by a wide margin in both categories. It scores almost 80% in the *most influential* category, with newspapers a distant second at 7.4%. And TV posts almost a 70% *most persuasive* score, with newspapers, again the runner-up, at 10.5%.

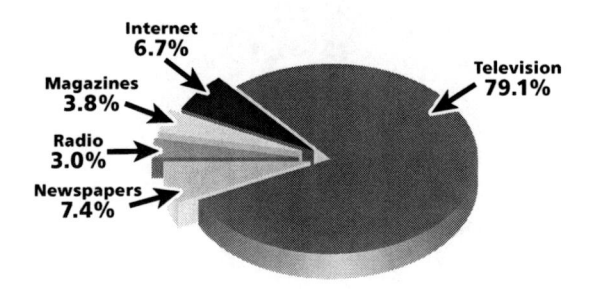

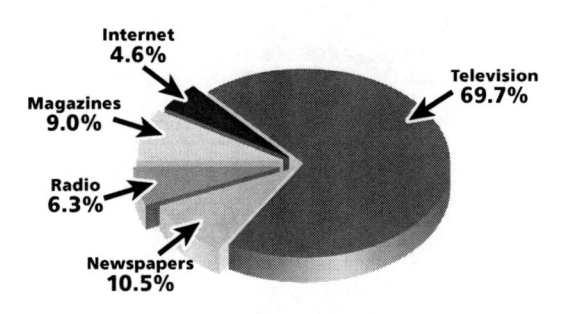

Television Advertising Has the Best Perception Among Adults

Most Influential

- Internet 6.7%
- Magazines 3.8%
- Radio 3.0%
- Newspapers 7.4%
- Television 79.1%

Television Bureau of Advertising 2009 TV Basis and TVB, Nielsen Media Research Custom Survey 2008

Television Advertising Has the Best Perception Among Adults

Most Persuasive

- Internet 4.6%
- Magazines 9.0%
- Radio 6.3%
- Newspapers 10.5%
- Television 69.7%

Television Bureau of Advertising 2009 TV Basis and TVB, Nielsen Media Research Custom Survey 2008

NUMBER ONE SOURCE FOR LEARNING ABOUT PRODUCTS

For advertisers, TV remains the primary link to the American consumer. More than half the consumers (52.9%) say they are most likely to learn about products or brands they'd like to buy from television commercials. This is more than twice the number choosing Internet ads (17%), followed by magazine ads, newspaper ads and radio commercials.

More Adults Learn About Products and Brands from Television

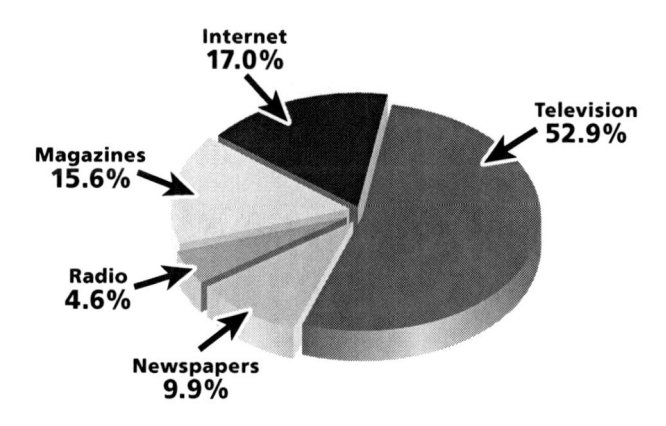

- Television 52.9%
- Internet 17.0%
- Magazines 15.6%
- Newspapers 9.9%
- Radio 4.6%

Television Bureau of Advertising 2009 TV Basis and TVB, Nielsen Media Research Custom Survey 2008

PRIMARY NEWS SOURCE

Broadcast television is the primary news source among adults. And when cable news networks are added to that number, no other medium comes close.

More Adults Say Broadcast Television is Their Primary Source of News

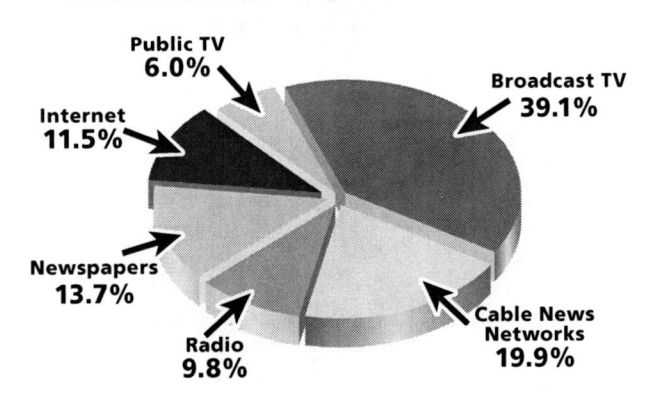

- Public TV 6.0%
- Internet 11.5%
- Newspapers 13.7%
- Radio 9.8%
- Broadcast TV 39.1%
- Cable News Networks 19.9%

Television Bureau of Advertising 2009 TV Basis and TVB, Nielsen Media Research Custom Survey 2008

First for Breaking News

All of the major demographics tell the same story: for breaking news, more adults turn to TV first compared with all other media.

More Adults Turn to Broadcast Television First for Breaking News

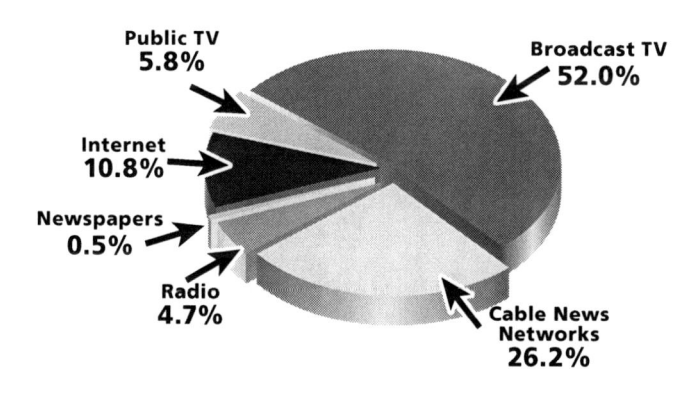

- Public TV: 5.8%
- Internet: 10.8%
- Newspapers: 0.5%
- Radio: 4.7%
- Cable News Networks: 26.2%
- Broadcast TV: 52.0%

Television Bureau of Advertising 2009 TV Basis and TVB, Nielsen Media Research Custom Survey 2008

FIRST FOR LOCAL WEATHER, TRAFFIC AND SPORTS

When it comes to getting the daily basics of weather, traffic and sports, viewers overwhelmingly turn to television.

More Adults Turn to Broadcast Television First for Local Weather, Traffic or Sports

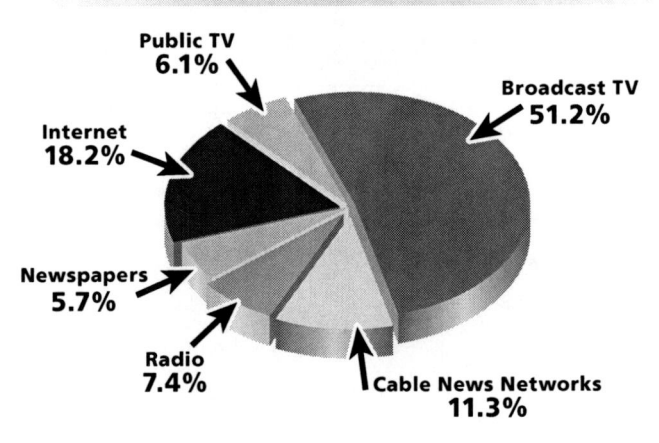

- Public TV 6.1%
- Internet 18.2%
- Newspapers 5.7%
- Radio 7.4%
- Cable News Networks 11.3%
- Broadcast TV 51.2%

Television Bureau of Advertising 2009 TV Basis and TVB, Nielsen Media Research Custom Survey 2008

MOST INVOLVED IN THE COMMUNITY

Television has built a solid reputation of commitment to important issues in local communities.

More Adults Feel Broadcast Television is Most Involved in Their Community

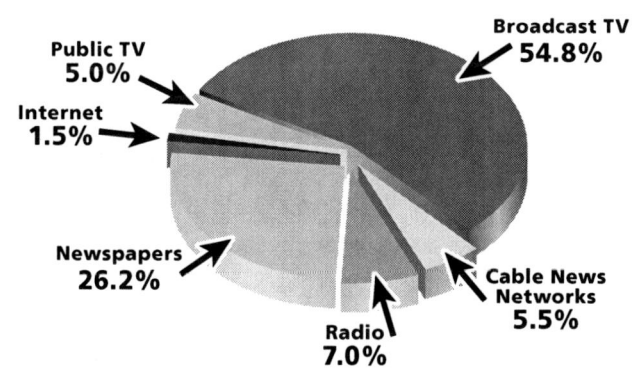

- Broadcast TV: 54.8%
- Newspapers: 26.2%
- Radio: 7.0%
- Cable News Networks: 5.5%
- Public TV: 5.0%
- Internet: 1.5%

Television Bureau of Advertising 2009 TV Basis and TVB, Nielsen Media Research Custom Survey 2008

There you have it. The pictures tell the story. In fact, in every category presented throughout this chapter, there is no other medium that comes close to having the impact and influence that television has on our society. Whether it's news, sports, weather or entertainment, people's first choice is television. Haddon Robinson makes a very interesting observation about this:

> We do less and less reading today. Often when you ask a pastor, "What do you have to do to develop as a Christian?" one of the things he'll say is, "Well, you have to study the Bible." But the Bible is a tough read. The generation I grew up in really valued reading. But I think that today a person who wants to be an effective communicator has to have an awareness of visual media like movies and what goes on in television, because that's the way people get their information. The average person spends about 200 hours a year reading the newspaper, about 200 hours a year looking at magazines, and 1,300 hours a year watching TV. When people are asked what is their major source of news, they say television; 55 percent say it's their only source of news. So they're being shaped by a [medium] that is visual and that tells stories.[19]

As communicators, we have to ask why. What makes television so influential? What keeps people tuned in for four or five hours a day? In the second half of the book, we will look at the communication principles that television adheres to and how we can implement these principles to effectively strengthen our own communication skills.

---

[19] Michael Duduit, "Expository Preaching in a Narrative World: An Interview with Haddon Robinson," *Preaching* 17, no. 1 (July-August 2001): 13. Please note that Haddon's figures date back to 2001, whereas mine are from 2008/2009.

Part Two

COMMUNICATION PRINCIPLES PREACHERS CAN LEARN FROM TELEVISION

3

WHO ARE YOU TALKING TO?

"You're foolish to try to have something for everyone, because then you have nothing for anyone."

—Andy Stanley—

The Apprentice and *American Idol* are two very successful television shows, yet they attract two completely different audiences. *The Apprentice* targets young professionals between the ages of 25 and 34, while *American Idol* primarily targets teens and young adults between 12 and 24. Before any television show ever hits the air, the producers determine what demographic they want to go after and find out as much information as they can about their target audience. Then they tailor the entire show to that audience, from the set design to the selection of the cast, wardrobe and script writing.

To put it simply, producers know that individual programs can't be all things to all people. This is why stations carry a wide selection of programs that appeal to a variety of people. For example, it shouldn't come as a surprise that the majority of viewers that watch NFL football are males 18 and older. And that the advertising during an NFL game will consist of cars, beer, fast food restaurants and home improvement commercials—all of which appeal to that program's target audience. In fact, the first question advertising agencies buying commercial airtime during a program ask is *Who does the show target?*

Likewise, the majority of viewers that watch *Dr. Oz* are females 30 and older. During his program you'll see commercials for diet programs, department stores, health and beauty items and a variety of food products that are strategically placed within the program to target his female audience.

Not only do stations carry certain programs that target a certain audience; over the years, the stations themselves have become more and more targeted, with stations like ESPN, sports all the time; CNN, where you get all news 24 hours a day; and HBO, where you can sit, eat popcorn and watch one flick after another, day and night. Whatever your interest, there's a station that delivers it 24 hours a day. There are hundreds of stations today specifically targeted with the one-niche format. In fact, programmers have taken all-sports stations one step further. We now have 24-hour NFL, NBA, NHL and golf stations, just to mention a few. And anyone interested in a particular format, whether it's sports, news, movies, food or home and garden, will watch that station more than any other, simply because it delivers that particular type of programming every hour on the hour, 7 days a week.

Who Are You Targeting?

Whether you're aware of it or not, your church is targeting someone. From the design of the building to the decor and layout of the sanctuary, the music played during worship, the design and layout of the handouts, and the way everyone dresses—everything is targeting a specific audience. *Who are you targeting?*

Bill Cosby said it best when he stated, "I don't know the key to success, but I know the key to failure is trying to please everybody." I have news for you: you can't target everyone, because you may not get anyone. In short, there is no way you can be all things to all people. There may be someone who doesn't like the decor of your building. Someone else may think your worship style is too old. Another may think the church pamphlet looks like something from pre-World War II and doesn't jive with the hip, glossy, four-color flyers they receive in the mail. The reasons why people may not be attending your church could be numerous.

During my research, I interviewed some of the biggest names in today's pulpits, and every time I got to this question about target audience, they had difficulty understanding what I was asking them—with the exception of one person. The rest all thought I was asking how they went about targeting their message, and they all answered something like, "Well, I make sure I have a word for everyone during the message." The question embraced much more than just the message; it embraced the entire essence of the church, including the name and logo, layout and decor of the building and the worship style. *Who are you as a church? Who are you appealing to? And how are you perceived, not only by the people who attend your church but, more importantly, by the people on the outside?*

Andy Stanley was the only one who fully understood the question, because he knows exactly who he's targeting:

> A great example is Walmart. I shop at Walmart. You probably go to Walmart. Everybody I know goes to Walmart. Do you know who Walmart's target audience is? They have one target audience.... It's the one grid through which they price, shelve and pick products. It's the guy that lives paycheck to paycheck. Now is that who they get? No. They get everybody. But they're smart enough to know you cannot market to more than one group at a time. You may get more than one group, but you're foolish to try to have something for everyone, because then you have nothing for anyone....
>
> And in terms of the audience who I'm speaking to, it's the 35-year-old guy who's married and has some young kids and is in business; that's the guy. Because if I can talk to the guy, whether it's the principle of the message or the application of the message, I'm going to get the whole family. The reason I'm targeting the guy is because the person that's most resistant to getting up on Sunday morning is that 35- to 40-year-old guy. He's got a measure of success. He's got options on Sunday. He's not against God. He's not even against Jesus, but we're taking a block of his time. And his time is precious because he works hard. He may be out of town a lot, and now he's think-

ing, "You want me to get up and get dressed and go somewhere? It better be good." And you know, it's not even a spiritual issue. It's a time issue. It's a priority issue. It's an "I got options" issue. So, I feel like if I can talk to that guy, he'll get his wife there.... And the women in turn will get their children there....

So the question I think every church needs to ask is *Who is our target audience?* We've got one, and every church needs to figure out who that is, because they're marketing to somebody. And if they don't know who, they can't measure the results or change. And if they're afraid to decide who, that's unfortunate, because they are marketing to somebody, whether it's a demographic issue, an age difference, an income, you know, there's some group they are most appealing to, and I think that's an important conversation to have.[20]

How Do You Know Who to Target?

There are several ways. In television, before producers decide to produce a show, they assess the television landscape and find out if there are any similar programs already on the air. Also, they produce a pilot of the program and show it to a focus group from the target audience to find out their reactions, thoughts and opinions. The feedback they receive from this group will determine what modifications, minor or major, they make to the program.

These focus groups, which are usually made up of six to 12 individuals are conducted by a mediator, who is in the room with the selected group while all the interested parties (producers, directors, writers, etc.) are in an adjacent room separated by a one-way window. They can see and hear the focus group, but the group can't hear or see them and is never told that the producers are watching and listening. It's done this way because the producers want to witness firsthand not only every verbal reaction, thought and opinion but every non-verbal response as well. Participants are asked various open-ended questions,

---

[20] Personal interview with Andy Stanley, 2 August 2005.

which are designed to stimulate thinking, rather than specific responses. A well-run focus group can deliver relevant qualitative research. A skilled interviewer can move beyond the immediate question and response to delve deeper and determine what the person is thinking when making a particular response.

Can you imagine gathering a group of people in your area and having a mediator ask them a number of questions about church and their individual church experiences while you're sitting behind a window, watching and hearing all of it? How beneficial do you think that exercise would be in finding out your target audience's needs?

A second, less intense but statistically informative way to gather information about the people in your immediate area would be to do a survey. Your local post office or township office has a wealth of information that can be easily retrieved for a nominal fee, and it's worth every penny. It includes how many people live in a particular home, their ages, incomes, nationalities and occupations. It's really up to you how detailed you want the information to be.

A final suggestion would be to do what Rick Warren did. When Rick started Saddleback Community Church, he knocked on over 500 doors in the area, wanting to find out why people didn't go to church. To his surprise, he found that the number one reason was because the sermons were boring and irrelevant. He quickly decided to seriously re-examine his preaching. He said to himself, "Whatever else happens, I've got to have messages that really meet the needs of the people and really help them in their daily life."[21] Rick had been involved in ministry for at least 15 years, and he had at least 10 years of sermons stockpiled. He could have easily coasted for quite a long time during the early years of Saddleback. Instead, he reviewed each sermon with one question in mind: *Would this message make sense to the unchurched people I just talked to?* It didn't matter whether Rick thought the message was good, or if it was homiletically correct or doctrinally sound, or if all the points started with the letter *p*. If he was going to start a church by attracting the peo-

---

[21] Rick Warren, "How to Communicate to Change Lives—Part 1," *Preaching Today*, cassette no. 120.

ple that he had spoken to, his messages would have to be messages that they could relate to. He ended up throwing out all but 3 of the sermons he had written in the previous 10 years. In essence, because Rick was interested in targeting the unchurched, he made the decision to tailor his communication style to attract that particular group.

Did it work for him? You better believe it did. Today, the church has grown to more than 50,000 members.[22] And one of the main things that contributed to that growth was Rick knowing exactly who he was after. He and the church's other leaders created a detailed picture of the kind of people they were trying to reach, and they even went so far as to give them names—Saddleback Sam and Saddleback Samantha.

> Saddleback Sam is the typical unchurched man who lives in our area [in the suburb of Irvine, California]. His age is late thirties or early forties. He has a college degree and may have an advanced degree. He is married to Saddleback Samantha, and they have two kids, Steve and Sally.
>
> Surveys show that Sam likes his job, he likes where he lives, and he thinks he's enjoying life more now than he was five years ago. He's self-satisfied, even smug, about his station in life. He's either a professional, a manager, or a successful entrepreneur.
>
> Another important characteristic of Sam is that he's skeptical of what he calls "organized religion." He's likely to say, "I believe in Jesus. I just don't like organized religion."[23]

The profile goes much deeper by including Sam and Samantha's tastes in pop culture, their preferences in social events, and so on. So what do these profiles do for Rick and the rest of his team? They give them a clear picture of the people they're trying to reach based on their research into who's living in the area.

---

[22] Chip Heath and Dan Heath, *Made to Stick: Why Some Ideas Survive and Others Die* (New York: Random House, 2007), 128.

[23] Ibid.

GETTING TO KNOW YOUR TARGET AUDIENCE

After you've decided the primary group you want to target, you need to get to know them. To speak to their felt needs, which we'll talk about more in the next chapter, you need to be aware of what those needs are. You need to walk in their shoes and see what they see, hear what they hear, and touch what they touch. In short, you need to know their world. There are several ways to do this. The following is not an exhaustive list in any way but just some suggestions to get you thinking.

Go to work with them. There's a very successful program called "Take Our Daughters and Sons to Work Day." The program is recommended for girls and boys ages 8 to 12 and in the U.S. is held every year on the fourth Thursday in April. On that day, parents take their children to work with them. I think it's a great program for several reasons. First, there's a bonding that takes place between parent and child. Second, the son or daughter becomes familiar with what his or her parent does, the people he or she works with, and the type of environment he or she works in. Finally, it expands the level of communication between parent and child.

I know several pastors who take advantage of this kind of exercise, but instead of taking their children to work, they go to work with members of their congregation. They might choose one person a month or every couple of months, or one person per quarter, and spend the day with him, seeing where he works and what he does.

This task should be done on an ongoing basis. I would recommend that you pick people from different occupational backgrounds. Go to work with an accountant, lawyer, dentist, plumber, chef, teacher, carpenter—the occupations in any given congregation are numerous.

Would an experience like that help you get to know the people who attend your church every week? Do you think it would help you communicate more effectively to your people? It's easy for pastors to become cocooned in their studies with the Amalekites and Perizzites and Hittites while the people in their pews are fighting their own "Canaanites," whether it's at work or in their marriages or families.

This is a great vehicle to get to know the people you speak to every week and find out who and what those Canaanites are.

Read everything you can get your hands on. If you want to get to know who you're speaking to every week, read what they read.
- Read the newspaper. Billy Graham often said that he read the newspaper in one hand and his Bible in the other. And during his messages, he often mentioned current events and people in the news.
- Be aware of what's on the *New York Times* best-seller list. And make sure you buy and read the books that are on there for long periods of time, whether it's a Harry Potter book or *The Da Vinci Code*.
- Read magazines. And when you come across articles that really grab your attention, tear them out and file them. They make for great illustrations, and, more importantly, it says to your people that you're "in the know" about what's going on in the world. So, read, read, read and keep on reading.

Watch TV. If you want to find out where people are and what's on their minds, watch the shows they're watching.

- Watch at least one newscast per day. You need to know at all times what's going on at home and around the world.
- Be aware of the current popular sitcoms. Watch an episode of each and become familiar with the characters and the issues they deal with.
- One area of television programming that has really taken off is reality TV. Become familiar with those programs and the challenges that the contestants face.
- Watch news magazine and documentary-type programs like *60 Minutes*, *Dateline* and *20/20*. They are great resources for finding out what people are thinking.
- Watch at least a couple of episodes a month of an entertainment-based program to keep up on what's happening in Hollywood. I prefer to watch *Entertainment Tonight*, but there are others like *Access Hollywood* or *The Insider*. Everybody wants to live the Hollywood life, and there are people who know more about their favorite singer or actor than they know about their own family members.

- I suggest you make a pit stop every once in a while and watch one of the music video channels, in order to be aware of some of the latest music videos, as well as the types of promotions and even talk shows these channels air to target today's teens.
- Finally, you can't overlook daily television talk shows, an excellent resource for finding out what's hot and what's not in today's world. Shows like *Oprah, Dr. Phil* and *Larry King* not only have millions watching, they also have a tremendous influence.

Go to the movies. Millions and millions of dollars pour into movie box offices every week. And not a week goes by without new movies being released.

A pastor I know thinks the movie theatre is not a place for the men and women of God. And because of that, he chose not to go see *The Da Vinci Code*. He said, "I want to be the only person who chooses not to go watch that movie." I believe he is doing a disservice to the people he speaks to. During that whole *Da Vinci Code* book and movie craze that swept not only the nation but the entire world, you couldn't pick up a newspaper or magazine or listen to a radio show without something being said about it. And that doesn't include all of the TV programs and Web sites that presented facts, argued or defended the contents of the book or commented on the movie. When something is that big, you can't ignore it. There may be people coming to church expecting to hear something about the issue. And I believe it's our duty as men and women who speak for God to defend what is true and what is not in a case like that. I can't count how many conversations I had both with churched and unchurched people about questions they had after reading the book or watching the movie—talk about an open door!

Listen to the radio. Radio has been greatly transformed over the years. Up until the late '80s and early '90s, you could tune in to your favorite radio station and hear a little bit of everything—music, news, sports, weather—all on one station. Today, that has changed. You now have 24-hour all-news stations, all-sports stations, all-talk stations, and the list goes on. If you want to know what's on people's minds, tune in to the all-news and all-talk formats. The all-talk formats have call-in shows with different hosts throughout the day. These are excellent resources for finding out what people are thinking.

Walk the mall. The mall is a great location for observing people. Try sitting in the food court and watching all that takes place around you. Notice what people are eating, how they're dressed, how they walk, how they talk—it's a great place to check the pulse of society.

Make the most of every conversation. I recently had a conversation with a 20-year-old girl who was preparing to go into her first year of college. I mentioned that we used to listen to music on vinyl records. Well, she made me feel as if I was from Abraham's era because she had no idea what I was talking about. With an odd look on her face, she said, "What are vinyl records?" I stood there, stunned at the thought that this girl, who was carrying around an iPod smaller than the size of a credit card that could store thousands of songs, had never seen a turntable with a vinyl record spinning on it. Conversations like that make for perfect illustrations of how rapidly things in our society change and how things that we used to use or be dependent upon just a short decade or two ago are obsolete today.

These are just a few ways to get to know your audience every week. You need to remember that in the end, it all comes down to how well you know your world and how well you understand the people you're trying to reach. Not only do you have to be knowledgeable of the Scriptures, you also have to be knowledgeable of your audience and the world they live in.

> If we do not know what is taking place in the culture, if we do not understand the winds that sweep across us, if we do not know what is fashioning and shaping the people in that society on every level, then there is no chance that churches are going to be able to speak into the lives of people. To think strategically means that you see what is going on. You know the Bible, but you're able to bring it to bear on life. You have to understand what television and movies and the media do to

people. We need to know the messages that come again and again disguised as a word from the sponsor. We need to know what is shaping and molding the people of our country.... We must change or we will discover that we are totally irrelevant to the culture in which we live.... We are called to minister in this day to the people in our culture.[24]

I love what David Henderson says in his book *Culture Shift* about the need to know your audience:

> If you know your audience like you know your Bible, God's Word will hit home to the heart and lightning will strike. Know your surrounding world like a meteorologist knows the shape of the clouds, like a gardener knows the texture of the soil, like a mechanic knows the purr of an engine, like a mother knows the voice of her child. Be an ardent student of your world.[25]

ONCE YOU KNOW WHO YOUR TARGET AUDIENCE IS...

As you become a student of your world and define who it is you're after, it will affect every part of your church. Here are just some of the key areas that would definitely be affected, followed by some initial questions to get you thinking.

When you know who your target audience is, it will affect...

The layout and decor of your sanctuary. Do you keep the hard wooden pews, or do you go with cushioned chairs? Do you go with stained glass windows? Do you keep all the sanctuary lights on full during the service, or do you dim them down to half? Or are the lights turned down completely and the platform is the only thing that remains lit? Do you keep the big "pope" chairs on the platform? Do you use a pulpit, or do you remove it?

---

[24] Robinson, "Our Mission in a Changing World."
[25] David Henderson, *Culture Shift: Communicating God's Truth to Our Changing World* (Grand Rapids, MI: Baker Books, 1998), 221.

Your style of worship. Do you keep the gowned 40-member choir? Do you focus on hymns or contemporary music? If you're thinking, *Well, what if I do both?* I can tell you firsthand it won't work. You're going to have to choose one or the other. And on that note, do you introduce an orchestra, or do you get rid of the orchestra and introduce a 5-piece band that includes drums and a complete percussion section?

The graphics you show on your overhead screens. Will you be creative and use a variety of fonts, colors and special effects, or will it have a unified look with very little color that robotically slides one message after the other?

The design and look of your handouts. Will the handouts be in black and white with all the information off-center and look like they were photocopied on the church photocopier that's been around as long as the church? Or will they be printed in four colors on good paper stock and be as appealing to the eye as possible? Will people receive just one handout when they come in? Or will there be other loose papers included in that handout, one announcing the rummage sale, one for the prayer meeting, one for the men's breakfast and one for the ladies' retreat?

The way you dress. Will you continue to wear the robe? What about the collar? Will you wear a suit, or will you go for a more casual look?

The way you deliver your message. Do you stand behind a pulpit, or do you walk around? Or do you use a pulpit at all? Do you stand, or do you sit? (Now there's an interesting question.) Do you shout a lot, or do you speak in a conversational tone that people are used to? Do you speak in a "churchy" stained-glass holier-than-thou voice, or do you just be yourself?

The language you use. Do you use religious jargon, or do you choose words everybody understands that communicate the same meaning? Do you explain the meaning of Greek and Hebrew words? Which version of the Bible will you use? Will it be the King James Version or the New Living Translation?

As you can see, when you know who it is you're targeting, it will affect every single area of your church. In fact, it will help align all areas of your ministry towards your target audience. This will ultimately force you to make some very difficult, but important, decisions.

So, who are you targeting? If you're looking for any significant progress or change to happen in your ministry, it won't happen until you take the time to sit down and answer that question as clearly as you can. Then, more importantly, decide to do something about it. Until you do, everything will remain the same.

Close-Up Shot

- You can't be all things to all people.
- Find out who you want to target.
- Get to know as much about them and their worldview as you can.
- Tailor every area of your ministry to target that particular audience.

4

ON THE AIR

"I think when people come to church they sit there with clickers in their heads. They turn you on or they'll turn you off. People will decide in the first 30 seconds if you're going to be interesting or boring. That's why an introduction today carries such important weight."

—Haddon Robinson—

If you were around in the '70s, I'm sure you'll remember these lyrics to the introductory theme song of one of television's most-watched sitcoms (situation comedies):

> Sunday, Monday, Happy Days.
> Tuesday, Wednesday, Happy Days.
> Thursday, Friday, Happy Days.
> Saturday, what a day,
> Groovin' all week with you...[26]

You may have noticed that since *Happy Days* first went to air in

---

[26] Norman Gimbel and Charles Fox, "Happy Days," performed by Pratt and McClain, original air dates: 1974-1984 on ABC, <http://www.cfhf.net/lyrics/happy.htm>, accessed 11 February 2006.

1974, a lot has changed in the way television programs are introduced. Back then, whether it was *The Brady Bunch, Gilligan's Island, Welcome Back Kotter* or *Little House on the Prairie*, a show would begin with its theme music, photos of the cast and the names of the producer, director and writers. Today, whether you're watching *Law & Order SVU* or a rerun of *Friends*, the action begins immediately. No intro theme music, no cast photos, no credits—just action, right off the top. If you miss the introduction, you'll miss the murder they're trying to solve or the situation they're trying to deal with.

It's only after the introduction to the plot that the theme music plays and the credits are shown. The same elements are still there, but the order has been reversed. First, they hook you with the "who done it" question, in the case of a *Law & Order* episode, then they segue into the show's intro, followed by the first commercial break. Why? The answer is simple: to get your attention as quickly as possible so that you won't click your remote and go off to watch some other program. Television producers work hard at making the introductions to their programs as compelling as possible to hook you as fast as they can.

Have you noticed how movies begin these days? They no longer waste time identifying in big bold letters the main stars or the director, producer or screenwriter. You get all of that information at the end of the movie. At the beginning there is perhaps a quick flash of the movie's title, if that, and then it's action! Whether it's a movie or television program, the same principle applies: introductions need to engage the audience immediately.

ATTENTION, INTEREST, NEED

On any given Sunday morning, you are trying to get and keep people's attention. Ultimately, you're trying to take their voluntary attention and turn it into involuntary attention,[27] to take the attention they give you because they have to, or are obligated to, and turn it into the attention they give you because they want to.

---

[27] Haddon Robinson, "How Can I Speak So An Audience Will Listen?" Tyndale Seminary, 13 June 2000.

The truth is, capturing attention is difficult. The difficulty with focusing solely on attention is that it's very short-lived:

> This is the way attention works. It fades in and fades out. It flits from one stimulus to another, incessantly. We can give our primary focus to only one stimulus (or group of stimuli) at a time, and we can hold it there for only a few seconds; then it must shift. So attention is very transient and unstable, moving now to this, now to that, and now to something else. Every moment we are awake, we constantly and inevitably focus our attention upon one thing after another, either within ourselves or within our environment.[28]

Haddon Robinson adds:

> Social scientists say that when you're driving a car, the focus of your attention can change as much as 200 times a minute. In fact, even while sitting, listening to a speaker, the focus of one's attention can change five to six times a minute. The reason for that is, a person can think five times faster than a person can speak. So there's a lot of dead air that a speaker is not able to fill, which in turn makes attention a very fleeting thing.[29]

Therefore, even though our desire as speakers is to get and keep people tuned in, we can't concentrate just on getting their attention. We have to go deeper and aim at their interest. If we can touch a person's interest, we can focus his attention because we tend to give our attention to things that we're interested in.

Two Friends

I have a friend who loves old cars. He goes to car shows all across the United States to see what's out there and what he can buy. And every time I see him, he can't stop talking about the latest car show

---

[28] Duane Litfin, *Public Speaking: A Handbook for Christians*, 2nd ed. (Grand Rapids, MI: Baker Book House, 1992), 46.
[29] Robinson, "How Can I Speak So An Audience Will Listen?"

he attended or the car that he's working on. I also know someone who's an art lover. She enjoys spending hours and hours in museums. Whether it's the Louvre in Paris or the Metropolitan Museum of Art in New York City (she's been to both), she'll be roaming the halls, wide-eyed, jaw unhinged, taking it all in. Both give their attention to what they are most interested in. Interest is longer lasting than attention; it's more basic. It's not as transitory. It doesn't bounce around as much.

There is one more rung on the ladder that goes a little higher than interest, and that's need. We are usually interested in what we need and we give our attention to what we are interested in.[30]

Jerry Weissman, former TV producer and screenwriter who now coaches CEOs in how to deliver speeches, says that you shouldn't dance around the appeal for self-interest. He says that WIIFY—"what's in it for you," pronounced *whiff-y*—should be a central aspect of every speech. What matters most to people is themselves. So it should come as no surprise that the most reliable way to make people care about what you're talking about is by invoking their self-interest[31]—by speaking to a need in their lives. Bill Self perhaps said it best:

> I really don't think that the man in the pew—the secular man—is hungry to know "what the Bible says." He is hungry for control of his life, hungry to get his life straightened out, hungry to "get his itches scratched." Biblical preaching is taking that point of need and leading the needy to the source of help—the Bible.[32]

What we need determines what we're interested in. And what we're interested in determines what we give our attention to. Attention, interest and need are three essential elements for every good introduction.

---

[30] Haddon Robinson, "Speaking from a Listener's Point of View," Gordon-Conwell Theological Seminary, 1991.
[31] Heath and Heath, *Made to Stick*, 177, 179.
[32] R. Albert Mohler, "Preaching to Joe Secular: An Interview with William E. Self," *Preaching* 4, no. 3 (November-December 1988): 3.

A Good Introduction Gets Attention

A good introduction immediately engages the audience. You won't be able to get their interest and speak to their needs unless you first get their attention. The minute you open your mouth to speak you should strive to get it as quickly as possible. How do you do it as quickly and as effectively as television?

Let's take a walk through the first half of a typical Sunday morning 11:00 service. First, an associate pastor welcomes everyone. Then, the service is turned over to the worship pastor and his team, and the singing begins. After that, the associate pastor prays an opening prayer. Next, the congregation sits through announcements, read like a shopping list. They're reminded of the Wednesday night Bible study and the yard sale on Saturday morning, and they're given an update on when the roof will be reshingled. Once the announcements have been taken care of, the associate pastor proceeds with a prayer for the offering, which is then collected. It's now about 11:30, and it's finally your turn to get up and speak.

That really is a tough act to follow. You'd better have something good to say, or you've already lost them before you even begin.

The Lead-In

When the people in charge of television programming are compiling their schedules, they pay a lot of attention to the lead-in program, the show that airs before each program. Suppose *Dancing with the Stars* airs at 8:00 p.m. and *Grey's Anatomy* airs at 9:00 p.m. *Dancing with the Stars* is the lead-in to *Grey's Anatomy*. When a new program debuts on one of the major networks at the start of a new season, usually in September, the cast and crew of that new show hope and pray that they will be placed after a strong lead-in. Why? Because they hope that the loyal audience watching that particular lead-in program will stay tuned to watch the new program that follows.

In television, audience retention is everything. The audience ratings for a program determine how much the network can charge for its commercial airtime, and whether or not the show stays on the air or gets cancelled. If the show delivers poor audience ratings, that affects the bottom line and the program gets axed. It's as simple as that. And they do it at a moment's notice. Therefore, the networks strategically schedule each program so that the lead-in program will complement and maintain audience ratings for the show that follows. They strive to create a synergy, a flow, from one show to the next.

A perfect example that demonstrates the importance of a strong lead-in is highlighted in what has been called the biggest mistake in TV history when NBC decided to move Jay Leno to 10:00 p.m. weeknights, and place Conan O'Brien as the new host of *The Tonight Show* at 11:30 p.m. NBC was hoping Leno would be a strong lead-in to the 11:00 p.m. news and Conan would attract a younger audience at 11:30 p.m. and give CBS's late-night king David Letterman a run for his money. Unfortunately, for NBC that never happened. Just a few short months later, NBC watched their ratings plummet. The move cost the network millions of viewers and advertising dollars to go to competing networks, simply because Leno's audience never moved with him to his new 10:00 p.m. time slot. Not only did Leno's show turn out to be a poor lead-in to the all-important 11:00 p.m. late-night news, but Conan's viewership never ended up being what NBC had hoped for, allowing Letterman to further dominate in the late-night ratings. The result of all this? NBC immediately took action on their blunder and moved Leno back to hosting *The Tonight Show* at 11:30 p.m. and reprogrammed the 10:00 p.m. hour with strong lead-in shows for the 11:00 p.m. news. As for Conan, he was dropped by the network, but not after receiving a personal pay-out of more than 30 million dollars. Not a bad way to lose your job. The moral of the story? Strong lead-ins matter!

Years ago, a commercial break would separate the end of one program and the beginning of the next. Some stations still do that. But in most cases, they've deleted that commercial break because the networks don't want to risk people channel surfing between programs. That's why today one show ends and the other immediately begins. So, the next time you watch CNN and you see Larry King end his show and say his goodbyes, watch carefully. You'll notice that his final words are "Now stay tuned; *Anderson Cooper 360°* begins right now!" And the Anderson Cooper show begins. No commercial break between programs. No interruptions. One show ends and the other begins. Again, this is done because television strives to keep things moving. Their goal is to maintain a constant flow from one element to the next.

ACTION!

Now let's get back to Sunday morning, where your lead-in is made up of long prayers, a shopping list of announcements and the collection of money. With that kind of lead-in, you have to get people's attention quickly or you can consider them checked out even before you begin. So what should you do to get their attention the moment you open your mouth?

We have to take our cue from how television now does introductions. It's action right off the top. No intro theme music, no cast photos, no credits; the program simply begins. They don't want to waste any time, because they have literally seconds to play with and know you're holding a remote in your hand that can change the channel instantly.

The same is true on Sunday mornings. If you don't say something interesting immediately, your audience will check out. They may not be holding a remote in their hands, but they're definitely holding one in their heads.

> There's a lot of evidence that shows that the first 25 or 30 words you speak are among the most important words in the sermon. Because they are the beginning of a journey, people make up their minds very quickly whether this is going to be worth listening to or not. In fact, there have been some interesting studies recently that say that within the first 50 seconds—that's less than a minute—a congregation or an audience has decided whether you're going to be boring, or interesting, or whether it's worth their time to tune in.[33]

Watch one of the popular entertainment-based news magazine shows like *Entertainment Tonight* and note how they consistently intro-

---
[33] Robinson, "Speaking from a Listener's Point of View."

duce that program. During the 60-second intro they hit you every 7 to 10 seconds with a story they're going to cover in that half-hour show. They don't reveal any of the details but tease you to get your attention. Think of the first 30 seconds of your message as the equivalent of a "coming soon" movie trailer before the feature film at a movie theater.

You want to open your message with an interesting statement and make those opening words count:

> Your introduction may be the most important part of your message. It is the equivalent to a railroad conductor yelling, "All aboard!" Or in my case, it is the equivalent of standing beside our SUV, yelling, "Load up, we're leaving." The introduction should provide listeners with a reason to listen. Your introduction should raise the question you are going to answer, create the tension you are going to resolve, or point to the mystery you are going to solve. My impression is that many communicators, especially preachers, are so anxious to get into the body of their message they spend little time preparing their introductions. They leave the station alone.[34]

SUGGESTED OPENERS

The following list of suggested openers is not exhaustive by any means. The goal is to simply get you thinking of different ways you can grip your audience's attention immediately.

Advertisement. A print, radio, or TV ad that caught your attention. "The other day while I was stopped at a red light, I happened to look over at a bus shelter, and I saw an ad that read, 'Quick Divorce—$300. Call: 800-555-1234.'"

Familiar Saying. "'Sticks and stones may break my bones, but names will never hurt me.' How many of you have heard that saying? How many of you have used that saying? More importantly, how many of

---

[34] Andy Stanley and Lane Jones, *Communicating for a Change* (Sisters, OR: Multnomah Publishers, 2006), 153, 154.

you actually *believe* that saying? How many of you actually believe that sticks and stones hurt but names don't?"

Quotation. "During one of Larry King's interviews with Billy Graham, Larry asked Billy, 'What has surprised you most about your life?' And Billy Graham as quick as a flash answered, 'Its brevity.'"

Question. "Death. It's a subject that most people avoid talking about. In fact, it's a subject most people don't like talking about at all. But we're not going to avoid talking about it today. Because the question I have for you today is, have you ever thought of what happens to you the minute after you die?"

Song. "At the 1988 Grammy Awards, one song won three awards, for best record, best song and best vocal of the year. The song was sung by a gentleman named Bobby McFerrin. Some of you may know the song I'm speaking of, and others will recognize it instantly once I begin to read the opening lyrics. It became such a huge hit that it seemed that everyone you came across was either humming the tune or reminding you of its title if you weren't doing what it said. The song went like this:

> "Here's a little song I wrote,
> You might want to sing it note for note,
> Don't worry, be happy!"

You can either read the lyrics yourself, play that particular part of the tune, or even sing it, whichever you think will be most effective.

Statistic. "More than 25% or 53 million people in the United States participate in casino gambling."[35]

Story. People love stories. Whether you're 5 or 105, people enjoy hearing the words "Once upon a time...." One of the main reasons why television is so effective is because it's a story medium. Whether it's a sitcom or a documentary, television is in the story business. More impor-

---

[35] Thomas A. Garrett, "Casino Gambling in America and Its Economic Impacts," August 2003, 6, <http://www.stlouisfed.org/community/assets/pdf/casinogambling.pdf>, accessed 11 February 2006.

tantly, storytelling was Jesus' primary mode of communication. For a story to work well as an introduction, it needs to be clear, relevant and complementary to the main idea of the text that you'll be presenting.

Video Clip. Whether it's music, news, sports, a man-on-the-street interview or a movie scene, video clips are effective. They're a great way to communicate without saying a word. On-line video superstores that deal with church media include sermonspice.com, worshiphousemedia.com, shoutable.com and faithvisuals.com. There are also on-line boutique shops, such as bluefishtv.com, highwayvideo.com, worshipfilms.com and sermonvideos.com. For a complete list of visual resource sites and a description of what each offers, I recommend *Preaching* magazine's annual survey of visual resources.

The key is to make sure you get your audience's attention immediately. Engage them as quickly as possible with an unexpected element that makes them think *Tell me more. I want to hear more.* Or, *I didn't know that.* Or, *Really? That's interesting.*

> It's almost like talking to a group of preschoolers. You know you have to click your fingers and say, "Hey, hey, hey, everyone's attention up here!" because they're thinking about their schedules and everything else. One of the biggest sins I think preachers commit today is assuming that because they're there physically, they're there emotionally. And we cannot assume that. We can almost assume the opposite today—that even if they are there physically, they are not there emotionally—so we have to sort of get their attention.[36]

Turn in Your Bibles To...

Starting your message with "Turn in your Bibles to..." or "Last week we were in Acts 1, and this week we're in Acts 2" definitely doesn't work today.

---

[36] Michael Duduit, "Creating Messages That Connect: An Interview with Alan Nelson," *Preaching* 20, no. 6 (May-June 2005): 17.

I think preachers of the past made a lot of assumptions about their audience that we can't make today, assumptions that the people in front of them knew the Bible and were interested in hearing the Bible taught, so they would just dive into the middle of a text and say, "Today I want to talk about the decrees of God."[37]

Keith Willhite concurs:

Standards such as "Take your Bibles and turn to...," "This morning we continue our series in...," and "Thank you for that lovely ministry in song..." have resounded as the first words from the preacher's lips with a predictability that rivals the sun's rise. If all television dramas began the same way, we'd turn on the set five minutes after the hour, instead of on the hour. I wonder when people really "tune-in" to our sermons.[38]

Haddon Robinson had some very sobering words to share about this. "For people to sit before the Scriptures and believe that they are a dull and insipid book or to be introduced to Jesus Christ and respond with a wide yawn, that's not just a sin against truth; that's a sin against God."[39]

Starting a message with a joke doesn't always work either—especially a joke that has nothing to do with the message. When humor is used in a subtle and tasteful way, it not only helps alleviate some of the tension but more importantly helps drive home the main idea. But there is a huge difference between using humor thoughtfully and starting a message with a corny, useless, joke. Duane Litfin said it best: "Long-winded, lamely told, irrelevant, or distasteful jokes usually do far more harm than good."[40]

---

[37] Haddon Robinson, "Doing Introductions," *Pulpit Talk CD*, Winter 2003, vol. 1, no. 2.

[38] Keith Willhite, "A Sneak Peek at the Point: Sermon Introductions that Aim at Application," *Preaching* 5, no. 6 (May-June 1990): 17.

[39] Robinson, "How Can I Speak So An Audience Will Listen?"

[40] Litfin, *Public Speaking*, 247.

A Good Introduction Surfaces a Need

There is a law in communication called Cohen's Law, after Arthur Cohen, who developed it. Haddon Robinson calls this law "the John 3:16 of communication." It says, "Information that is given in response to a perceived need makes a deeper impact and lasts longer than information that is given and then applied."[41] Do you want your messages to have a lasting impact on the people that hear them? Then find out what their needs are and speak to those needs. It's really just that simple.

In short, a powerful message is one that deals directly with a felt need. And a felt need is found in the gap between what a person has or is dealing with and what that person needs. When you aim at need, you show people how what you're about to say will answer a question, solve a problem, head toward a goal or meet a desire. Therefore, a good introduction doesn't answer a question; it asks it. It doesn't solve a problem; it presents it.

> The sermon's issue of decision becomes clear when a human need becomes focused in a particular question that calls for some sort of resolution.... By the time my sermon introduction is finished, they should see clearly, perhaps even feel, their need. The heart of the listener who is directed to his or her need for God's truth is a heart sitting on the edge of its seat.[42]

Rick Warren said:

> By beginning with people's needs when you preach, you immediately gain the attention of your audience. Practically every communicator understands and uses this principle except pastors! Wise teachers know to start with the student's interests and move them toward the lesson. Effective salesmen know you always start with the customer, not the product. Smart managers know to begin with the employee's complaint, not their own agenda. You start where people are and

---

[41] Robinson, "Speaking from a Listener's Point of View."
[42] Willhite, "A Sneak Peek at the Point," 19, 20.

move them to where you want them to be.... Today, "preaching to felt needs" is scorned and criticized in some circles as a cheapening of the gospel and a sell-out to consumerism. I want to state this in the clearest way possible: beginning a message with people's felt needs is not some modern approach invented by 20th century marketing! It's the way Jesus always preached.[43]

Andy Stanley agrees:

Information that does not address a felt need is perceived as irrelevant. It may actually be incredibly relevant, but if our audience doesn't see or feel the need for it, it is perceived as irrelevant. No one is engaged. They may sit quietly until we are finished talking. But they will not be engaged.[44]

Need Creates Tension

"Tension is that agitated state of our nervous system that is called disequilibrium."[45] It's the thing that keeps you on the edge of your seat. It's the stuff that keeps you wanting more. Tension is all about an intense appetite on the part of the listener to keep on listening. And the only way to establish that tension is to surface a need. No need, no tension. Or, as Andy Stanley says, "You pay attention when there is tension.... Tension gains attention."[46]

Andy explained it to me this way:

Introductions are all about creating a tension that's so intense that people don't dare leave until you resolve that tension. One of the big mistakes in preaching is that everybody is moving out of the garage, or moving out of the train station, and nobody is

---

[43] Rick Warren, "Preaching for Life Change: It's All in Learning to Preach Like Jesus," *Preaching* 19, no. 2 (September-October 2003): 12, 13.
[44] Stanley and Jones, *Communicating for a Change*, 153.
[45] Calvin Miller, *The Empowered Communicator: 7 Keys to Unlocking an Audience* (Nashville, TN: Broadman & Holman Publishers, 1994), 111.
[46] Stanley and Jones, *Communicating for a Change*, 155.

feeling any tension. So what's the point in following?...The introduction is all about creating a tension or asking a question where it gets everybody thinking, *Oh my God, I've been wondering.* Or, *I've never wondered. Gee, do I need to wonder? What about that?* Or, *Wow, that's something I would love to know how to do.* Or, *That's something I need to quit doing.* The question is *Where's the tension?* And if there is no tension, then you're about to answer a question that the average person isn't asking.[47]

The following introduction taken from Andy's message "When Things Seem Uncertain" illustrates this idea:

It's easy to follow Jesus when He answers your prayers, isn't it? And it's not so easy when He doesn't, is it? Some of you tonight, you have some prayer requests you've had for a long, long time. Every time you go to a prayer meeting, you raise your hand and everybody says, "I know." Because it's the same thing over and over and over. And doesn't it make you upset when you go to a prayer meeting or you get into your community group, small group, or your prayer group and people have their prayers answered? And then they look at you and you say, "Uh, uh, not yet. He still hasn't come back." Or, "He came back." Or, "I haven't heard from her." "Still don't have a job." "Still uncertain about what's going on."

Maybe this is just me, but it's very difficult to be certain about God when times are uncertain. It's difficult to maintain faith in God when circumstances are uncertain. And then you open the Bible, and I'm just being transparent, sometimes the Bible is not encouraging because it seems so easy in the Bible, right? I mean, there are all these miracles. Every time they had a problem, somebody had a miracle. Angels showed up, the doors were opened, the sea parted, and I'm thinking, you know, just one, if I could just have one of those, I think it would keep me going for a long, long time, wouldn't it? How about you?

---

[47] Personal interview with Andy Stanley.

Stop Preaching and Start Communicating

But I mean, when God gets quiet, it's hard to maintain sometimes. You know, as a Christian I know how to handle prosperity. I know how to do that. I know how to do answered prayer. I know how to respond when God shows up. I don't need anybody to help me with that. I got the joy, joy, joy, joy, way down in my heart when God has answered my prayer, right? But when it's a week, and two weeks, and three weeks, and it's a month, and it's a year, and things continue to be uncertain in my life and your life, whether it's a temptation or a relationship, there are times when you start saying, "God? Hello? Are You out…? Are You going…? Is it ever going to get better?" And then you begin to wonder, *Is God even with me? He seems to answer everybody else's prayers. He seems to be listening to everybody else. But is God really with me?* Tonight, I want to answer the question *What do you do in the midst of those uncertain times?*[48]

Wouldn't you be interested in hearing the rest of the message? Andy touched on a felt need that created some very strong tension, which in turn created an intense desire to keep listening.

There are three questions that Andy recommends you consider when developing your introductions:

- What is the question I am answering? What can I do to get my audience to want to know the answer?
- What is the tension this message will resolve? What can I do to make my audience feel that tension?
- What mystery does this message solve? What can I do to make my audience want a solution?[49]

A Good Introduction Tells 'Em, But Doesn't Tell 'Em

A good introduction creates an itch but doesn't let them scratch it until the end of the message. Andy's introduction very clearly states the

---

[48] Andy Stanley, "When Things Seem Uncertain," Ocean Grove Rally, 22 June 2002.
[49] Stanley and Jones, *Communicating for a Change*, 154.

subject of his message—the complete, definite answer to the question *What am I talking about?* It doesn't keep people guessing; it's clear that he's going to answer the question he poses: *What are we to do in those times in our lives when things seem uncertain?* That's the tell 'em or itch part of the equation.

What Andy doesn't do in the introduction is give them the answer. That's the don't scratch part. If he were to do that, he might as well go ahead and take his seat, because the sermon would be over. Why? Because the tension would be gone. And as Haddon Robinson puts it, "When the tension goes, the sermon ends."[50] Keith Willhite explains the importance of this idea:

> The introduction to a sermon must provide a hint of the issue of decision without giving the details, illustrations and complete expected response. Immediately, a listener knows what we are talking about and why they should listen.... We are not to tip our hand, we are to merely hint at how strong the cards are.... Introductions should entice the listener with God's answer. The body of the sermon delivers the answer, but the introduction creates a hunger for it.[51]

INDUCTION AND DEDUCTION DEFINED

I'm sure you're familiar with—and perhaps were even taught in seminary—this old outline from Preaching 101: Tell them what you're going to tell them, tell them and then tell them what you told them. The introduction spells out in detail what the structure of the message will be, the body unpacks the message, and the conclusion replays the points that were made. Can you imagine a television drama, a movie, or even a theater production giving a summary of the plot during the introduction? Instead, television programs, as well as movies and theater productions, are always presented inductively. They're never presented deductively.

---

[50] Haddon Robinson, *Biblical Preaching: The Development and Delivery of Expository Messages*, 2nd ed. (Grand Rapids, MI: Baker Academic, 2001), 172.
[51] Willhite, "A Sneak Peek at the Point," 18, 20.

Communicating inductively is basically asking a question during the introduction and then arriving at the answer toward the end of the message. Deductive communication is the direct opposite. You state the main idea in your introduction, and then prove, explain, or apply it throughout the message. The following triangle diagrams will help you visualize the difference. Simply ask yourself *Where's the point?* If the triangle is pointing up, it's deductive, because the main point is stated in the introduction. If the triangle is pointing down, it's inductive, because the main point is stated towards the end of the message.

Deductive Model

Main idea is fully stated in the introduction.

Main idea is explained, proven or applied throughout the message.

Inductive Model

A question is raised in the introduction.

Main idea is fully stated towards the end of the message.

ADVANTAGES AND DISADVANTAGES

The inductive approach directly reflects the way we live life. "Life that is healthy and interesting moves from expectation to fulfillment repeatedly."[52] It is all about knowing, but not knowing. You know the question, but you don't know the answer. And the question and answer are held together by a tension that is not removed until the end. I like to think of it as a high wire act at a circus. The performer starts at one end and slowly, step-by-step, walks over to the other end while hundreds of spectators below watch with baited breath to see if he will make it. It's that tension, that anticipation, that keeps people on the edge of their seats. The inductive approach creates and sustains the

---

[52] Fred Craddock, *As One Without Authority—Revised and with New Sermons* (St. Louis, MO: Chalice Press, 2001), 52, 53.

audience's interest through anticipation. It feeds the tension that needs to be resolved, and the resolution doesn't come until the end.

Haddon Robinson confirms this idea:

> In the past I would go to my study, and I would come out, and I would deliver to the people what the results of my study would be. Today, there is a greater tendency to let the congregation in on your study. So it leads to induction rather than deduction. You sort of take the listener along on the journey with you. I think there is more of that being done, and I think it is a good trend because I think we live inductively. We have experiences, and out of those experiences we draw conclusions.[53]

Ed Young Jr. agrees:

> It's okay to keep them wondering what's coming next or to build tension in the sermon. In fact, I recommend a lot of tension. You just need to give them enough direction to get them to the next sign. Every road sign leads to the next and gives hints as to the final destination. Effective communicators reveal the final destination at the end, building a case from the beginning as to why listeners should pay attention. You've got to give them a reason to listen, even if it is just to relieve the tension that you've built along the way. A good introduction can hook the audience and allow you to reel them in little by little until you have reached the final conclusion.[54]

Some say that beginning deductively and stating your big idea clearly and early in the introduction allows listeners to grab on to it. But that's actually a disadvantage, because you give away all the cookies at the start. The listeners can now sit back and enjoy their cookies. They can check out, because they feel they got the gist of what you

---

[53] Michael Duduit, "Expository Preaching in a Narrative World: An Interview with Haddon Robinson," *Preaching* 17, no. 1 (July-August 2001): 10.

[54] Ed Young Jr., "Keys to Creative Communication," *Preaching* 21, no. 6 (May-June 2006): 16.

want to say. You gave them their *Aha!* moment already. In short, the tension is gone. And what happens when the tension is gone? The message ends. The deductive approach gives away the climax, which in turn kills the message.

Robert McKee, a well-known screenwriter, knows something about the power of inductive communication:

> His screenwriting seminars play to packed auditoriums of aspiring screenwriters, who pay five hundred dollars a head to listen to his thoughts. *The Village Voice* described his course as "damned near indispensable not only for writers, but also for actors, directors, reviewers and garden-variety cinephiles." His students have written, directed or produced television shows such as *E.R.*, *Hill Street Blues* and *The X-Files*, and movies ranging from *The Color Purple* to *Forrest Gump* and *Friday the 13th*…. In McKee's view, a great script is designed so that every scene is a Turning Point. Each Turning Point hooks curiosity. The audience wonders *What will happen next?* And *How will it turn out?* The answer to this will not arrive until the Climax of the last act, and so the audience, held by curiosity, stays put.[55]

For the Pro-Deductive Communicator

Communicating deductively *can* be done effectively when the main idea fully stated in the introduction raises questions in the listeners' minds and forces them to think *I wonder what he means by that*. Or, *I don't get what he just said. I hope he explains it.* Or, *Is what he just said really true?* Or, *So what? What difference does what he just said really make in my life?* Then the deductive model can sustain listeners' attention throughout the message.

The following is an edited version of a deductive introduction by Don Sunukjian that effectively raises a key question in the listeners' minds:

---

[55] Heath and Heath, *Made to Stick*, 83.

Early in geometry we learned the shortest distance between two points is a straight line. That may be true in geometry, but as you and I consider what God is doing in our lives, we wonder if God doesn't think *The shortest distance between two points is a zigzag.* That is, we find ourselves at Point A, convinced that God intends to take us to Point B. And we can visualize a short straight-line path between these two points. But if God is really taking us to Point B, he must be on a zigzag path. Today, I want you to see that sometimes, with God, the shortest distance between two points is a zigzag.[56]

What does he mean, the shortest distance between two points is a zigzag? That's exactly the question Don spends the rest of the message answering. Deductive messages that raise questions in the listeners' minds can keep tension alive.

HUH? BEFORE AHA!

The *Aha!* experience is much more satisfying when it is preceded by the *Huh?* experience.[57] This is the advantage of the inductive structure.

Most biblical material is written inductively. Most parables and narratives build up to the main idea at the end of the passage. And the majority of the Bible is narrative. In fact, while reading the Bible, I find myself many times saying to myself that what I just read would make for a great movie script. And of course that has already been done. *The Ten Commandments* and Mel Gibson's blockbuster *The Passion of the Christ* are both examples of scripts coming directly from the pages of Scripture. So, in fact, the screenwriter was God Himself.

Since God's primary mode in giving us His Word is inductive,

---

[56] Keith Willhite and Scott M. Gibson, eds., *The Big Idea of Biblical Preaching: Connecting the Bible to People* (Grand Rapids, MI: Baker Books, 1998), 113, 114.

[57] Heath and Heath, *Made to Stick,* 81.

consider moving away from the deductive approach, which is as old as Aristotle. It simply doesn't reflect life and communication today.

So in your introduction, tell them what you're going to talk about in the form of a question. Get them to itch. Give them only a single chocolate chip. Let them think *Huh?* But don't give them the answer. Don't let them scratch. Wait to give them the entire cookie. Let them wait for their *Aha!* moment. Go inductive.

SOME FINAL THOUGHTS

When preparing your introduction, keep in mind these final suggestions:

Provide the biblical background of the text that you're going to speak from. Don't assume that your audience knows anything about it. Give them all of the literary, cultural, historical and geographical information necessary, in five to ten sentences—no more than a short paragraph. Your audience will appreciate the message that much more if they feel a certain level of comfort with the text. Television will never run a story without giving viewers the background in the introduction to provide a proper understanding of the whole story.

Keep it short. The average length of an introduction for a 60-minute television drama like *Law & Order SVU* is 2.5 to 3 minutes. The average introduction for a 30-minute sitcom is 1 to 1.5 minutes. For a 30-minute message, an introduction shouldn't last longer than 5 minutes. Once you've gotten the audience's attention, surfaced a felt need, introduced the subject and given a brief background of the text, the message needs to transition forward to the first move.

(We'll discuss moves more in Chapter 5. Briefly, moves are modules of thought that flow from one to the other. Using moves in your sermon instead of listing points allows you to appear more conversational rather than lecturing.)

Read the chosen text for the message after the introduction. By then, the audience will have a clear understanding of your subject and of the text's biblical background, and so they'll pace right alongside you.

Read the text inductively, one portion at a time. Don't read the text in its entirety or play biblical hopscotch from text to text to text. Read the portion that deals with the first move, or Roman numeral, in your message. When you transition into your second move, read the next portion of Scripture. This will complement the inductive approach to the message, and you'll all arrive at the end at the same time. Andy Stanley suggests the following:

- Highlight and explain odd words or phrases. Think of yourself as a navigator or tour guide.
- Voice your frustration or skepticism about the text. If it frustrates you, it is likely frustrating someone in your audience.
- Help the audience anticipate the main point of the text by saying things like "Okay, get ready, here it is...." " or "And then he drops the bomb...."
- Resist the urge to share everything you have learned in your research.[58]

It's been said that there are three types of communicators: those you *can't* listen to, those you *can* listen to and those you *must* listen to. During the introduction, your audience is going to quickly decide which kind of speaker is addressing them.[59] Make your introduction count.

---

[58] Stanley and Jones, *Communicating for a Change*, 159, 162. You will find a complete list of Andy's suggestions beginning on page 159 right through to page 162.

[59] Robinson, *Biblical Preaching*, 167.

Close-Up Shot

- 🎥 A good introduction gets attention.
- 🎥 A good introduction surfaces a need.
- 🎥 A good introduction tells 'em but doesn't tell 'em.

5

Let's Talk

*"What is irrelevant, in my opinion, is our style of communicating the Bible.
We tend to still use the style from 50 years back, which doesn't match who we're trying to reach today."*

—Rick Warren—

Whether it's the 6:00 evening news or one of the numerous daily talk shows, television is a very conversational and relational medium. Even the set designs, complete with coffee tables and couches, contribute to their laid-back conversational presentation. The guests drink coffee while they're being interviewed, and the viewing audience listens in, feeling like they're part of the chitchat. There may be millions of people watching a particular show, but each viewer feels as if he or she is the only one they're speaking to, because television has mastered the art of getting personal with its audience.

I believe what drives television's instant rapport with the audience is that they speak in a language the viewers understand and they do it in a conversational manner. In short, it's all about what they say—their choice of words—and how they say it—their delivery—the *what* and the *how*.

Watch Your Language

When I first started attending church, I couldn't understand a word the preacher was saying. It was as if he were speaking a secret code to only the few select fortunate people who understood it. There were more Sundays when I left church confused than Sundays when I actually got something out of the message.

The KJV Fan Club

The first church I attended used the King James Version of the Bible exclusively. Everyone, including the pastor, truly believed that the KJV was the most accurate translation and that no other version came close. When I brought a different version with me because I couldn't understand what was being read, let alone said, it was like breaking the 11th commandment.

Today, I use the New Living Translation because of the everyday common language that's simple to understand. Check out the difference for yourself:

King James Version—Genesis 6:14-16:

> [14]Make thee an ark of gopher wood; rooms shalt thou make in the ark, and shalt pitch it within and without with pitch. [15]And this is the fashion which thou shalt make it of: The length of the ark shall be three hundred cubits, the breadth of it fifty cubits, and the height of it thirty cubits. [16]A window shalt thou make to the ark, and in a cubit shalt thou finish it above; and the door of the ark shalt thou set in the side thereof; with lower, second and third stories shalt thou make it.

New Living Translation—Genesis 6:14-16:

> [14]Make a boat from resinous wood and seal it with tar, inside and out. Then construct decks and stalls throughout its interior. [15]Make it 450 feet long, 75 feet wide and 45 feet high. [16]Construct an opening all the way around the boat, 18 inches below the roof. Then put three decks inside the boat—bottom, middle and upper—and put a door in the side.

King James Version—Philippians 4:6,7:

> ⁶Be careful for nothing; but in everything by prayer and supplication with thanksgiving let your requests be made known unto God. ⁷And the peace of God, which passeth all understanding, shall keep your hearts and minds through Christ Jesus.

New Living Translation—Philippians 4:6,7:

> ⁶Don't worry about anything; instead, pray about everything. Tell God what you need, and thank him for all he has done. ⁷If you do this, you will experience God's peace, which is far more wonderful than the human mind can understand. His peace will guard your hearts and minds as you live in Christ Jesus.

In both cases you can get a solid grasp of what's being said in the NLT passages with only one read-through, because it's reader- and listener-friendly. But you may have to read the same verses in the KJV a few times to figure out all that's being said. The NLT version translates outdated words like *pitch* and *cubits* into modern-day words like *tar* and *feet*, making it easy for people today to get a visual of what's being said.

For eight years, I did monthly prison chapel services, and at first I would read from the New American Standard Version, a close cousin to the KJV. And every time I would look up after reading a portion of Bible text, the inmates had an *I don't understand what you just read* look on their faces. When I switched to the NLT, their faces looked relaxed, their eyes were wide open, and they sat upright, which clearly communicated that they were tracking with me. Do your own experiment. During your family devotionals or in sharing something with a friend, read from the KJV, NKJV or NASB, and then read the same passage from the NLT, NIV, or the Good News Bible, and see what the reaction is. Without a doubt, they will prefer the more reader-friendly version that uses common everyday language. Why? Because that's the language they themselves speak and are used to hearing every day. So why muddy the communication of God's Word with a translation that's difficult to understand?

With more than 11 million copies sold, *The Message* by Eugene Peterson has been one of the most popular Bible translations of recent years because of its effort to translate biblical language into contemporary American speech. Eugene says the way he preached shaped the way *The Message* came out.

> I never thought of myself as a translator. I was always trying to translate—I was having this war between American culture and the Hebrew and New Testament cultures and wondering: *how can I say this? If Isaiah had been in my pulpit how would he say this?* That is what was going on in my head all the time.[60]

Does Anyone Have a Dictionary?

Just as frustrating as a hard-to-read Bible version are words that people have never heard before or are only spoken at church. I'm speaking of abstract theological words like *justification, propitiation, redemption, sanctification* and many others that we hear from the pulpit that very few understand. So why use them? Instead, use words or terms people do understand that say the same thing. It really comes down to making those abstract theological words concrete and specific, allowing people to engage all five senses to clearly understand what's being said.

> Concrete language helps people, especially novices, understand new concepts. Abstraction is the luxury of the expert. If you've got to teach an idea to a room full of people, and you aren't certain what they know, concreteness is the only safe language…. This is how concreteness helps us understand—it helps us construct higher, more abstract insights on the building blocks of our existing knowledge and percep-

---

[60] Michael Duduit, "Understanding the Word: An Interview with Eugene Peterson," *Preaching* 23, no. 3 (November-December 2007): 24.

tions. Abstraction demands some concrete foundations. Trying to teach an abstract principle without concrete foundations is like trying to start a house by building a roof in the air.[61]

But if concreteness is so powerful, why is it so easy for us to slip into abstraction? The answer is simple: because the difference between an expert and a novice is the ability to think abstractly.

It can feel unnatural to speak concretely about a subject matter we've known intimately for years. But if we're willing to make the effort we'll see the rewards: our audience will understand what we're saying and remember it.... The moral of the story is to find a "universal language," one that everyone speaks fluently. Inevitably, that universal language will be concrete.[62]

And so if the universal language is to be concrete, how do we accomplish it? We do so by using illustrations:

Illustrations tend to take an abstract concept and ground it into life. And people think with pictures in their heads. They don't think well with abstractions, so a good illustration helps to paint a picture in people's minds, so that it leads to clarity and understanding. The weak preachers are constantly saying "in other words." They made something unclear, and then they use other words to try and make it clear. The better preachers will tend to say "for example," "for instance," or "let me illustrate." So whenever you have an abstract statement, if you can follow it with a "for instance" or an example, a picture, an image, you have a better chance of communicating and thus a better chance of being clear.[63]

---

[61] Heath and Heath, *Made to Stick*, 104, 106.
[62] Ibid., 115.
[63] Haddon Robinson, "How to Bring Clarity to Sermons," *Seeking Unity*, Preaching Today, cassette no. 189.

As far as avoiding religious terms, Rick Warren says:

> A lot of pastors I know who aren't charismatic speak in an unknown tongue every week. And I would say this, using *big* words indicates a *big* insecurity. I find that people who have to impress you with their fancy words usually are very insecure people. The fact is, people don't talk in religious terms or spiritual terms anymore. They use psychological terms to describe their feelings. They say things like "I'm coming apart," "I'm at the end of my rope," "I'm about to pop," "I'm coming unglued." That's pop psychology. They don't say, "I'm experiencing total moral depravity." They just don't use terms like that. What they mean is "My life's messed up." But if you're going to communicate to the unchurched, you must say it in a sentence. You must say it without religious terms.
>
> I love to teach theology on Sunday mornings to the unchurched, not ever telling them it's theology and without ever using theological terms. It's just kind of a little game with me. I've done series on the attributes of God—you know, immutability, omniscience, omnipresence. I've done a series on justification, a series on the incarnation; I did a series on sanctification for 12 weeks and never even used the word. Not one time. I talked about God's part and my part in changing me. When I'm with my people, I say, "Jesus wants to be the CEO of your life. He wants to be the chairman of the board. He wants not just to be resident; He wants to be president." I often say the definition of a Christian is a sign that says, "Under New Management." Or, I'll say, "Let Jesus Christ be the manager of your life." Now my people can relate to that. They don't know what *Lord* is. We've never had lords and ladies in our society.[64]

Robert Jacks, author of *Just Say the Word*, tells a story of a seminary faculty member who was preaching in a black church in Trenton, New

---

[64] Rick Warren, "How to Communicate to Change Lives—Part 2," Preaching Today, cassette no. 121.

Jersey. Right in the middle of his sermon, a booming bass voice from the back of the church said, "Preacher, put those cookies on a lower shelf." Jacks goes on to say, "I think that's what people are asking for. To hear the word spoken to their lives in ways that they can understand it, in everyday language."[65] The key is to lower the cookie jar to a shelf where everyone can reach it.

WHAT LANGUAGE IS THAT?

When I was in seminary, I got into the habit of defining key Greek or Hebrew words from the passage I was preaching from. I heard others do it, so I did it, too. One day, one of the inmates came to me at the end of a prison chapel service and asked if I could see him at his cell. I finished gathering my things and then made my way there. I will never forget hearing him say, "I appreciate all the passion you bring to the chapel services, but you need to know one thing. Most of the guys in this place can't read or write. In fact, there are guys in here that are just learning the alphabet for the very first time in their lives. So when you start pronouncing Greek and Hebrew words, they don't have a clue what you're saying." It was one of the most humbling experiences I've ever had, and I have never mentioned another Greek or Hebrew word during any of my messages since. If it's hard enough for people to understand theological words in English, why use words in Greek and Hebrew? Ultimately, that's not what most people are interested in. People are interested in finding answers to life's daily challenges.

For thousands of years, before the alphabet and writing ever came on the scene, people communicated with pictures. So it's very clear that we have an innate attraction to them. When you come across a key word in a text that needs to be clarified, a word picture will help people visualize what that word means. It will have much more of an impact than pronouncing the word in its original language and defining it in abstract theological words that no one understands. Doing so

---

[65] Robert Jacks, "Preaching for the Ear," *True Holiness*, Preaching Today, cassette no. 190.

could also be perceived as puffing yourself up, flaunting your superior knowledge, and no one likes to feel inferior. Rick Warren said:

> Some pastors like to show off their knowledge by using Greek words and academic terms in preaching. Pastors need to realize that no one cares as much about Greek as they do. Chuck Swindoll once said that he believes an overuse of word studies discourages confidence in the English text. I agree.[66]

And Robert Jacks said it best:

> If we see ourselves as being in any respects superior to our people, even though we have a seminary degree, then I think that's going to have a terrible effect on our preaching. I have seen so many students who step into the pulpit and immediately they become "holy other," whether you spell that "wholly" or "holy," as though they had the word *God* stamped on their foreheads, as if they suddenly ascended to the top of the mountain.[67]

CHURCH IS NOT FOR CHURCH PEOPLE

Andy Stanley reminds us that "Church is not for church people. Church is for everyone." We should stop thinking that church is some kind of holy club where only those initiated understand the club's culture and language. In short, we have to stop feeding the already fed and instead reach out to those who are actually hungry. After all, isn't that what we're called to do? Ed Young Jr. shares a great story of the meaning behind this idea:

> Last summer I got in touch with my feminine side and took a day trip with my wife, Lisa, to the world's largest flea market, in a little town called Canton, Texas. That day, I watched in amazement as thousands of shopping fanatics, in triple degree Texas heat with perspiration dripping off their noses, pushed their shopping carts from shop to shop in hopes of finding the

---

[66] Warren, "Preaching for Life Change," 19.
[67] Jacks, "Preaching for the Ear."

deal of a lifetime. It was like sitting on the front row at an Olympic competition. If you've never been to Canton, there are truly not enough descriptive words in the English language to paint a picture for you of what it was like.

After two or three hours on the quest for the ultimate flea-market find, Lisa was kind enough to say, "Honey, let's break for some lunch." Grateful for the reprieve, I accepted her offer, and we made our way to the food area, which consisted of a group of rickety, wooden picnic tables strategically huddled around several food stands.

We bought a couple of chicken sandwiches at one of the restaurants and proceeded to one of the tables to eat. After a few minutes, Lisa looked over my shoulder and said, "Honey, check that out." As I turned, I noticed an employee of the restaurant carrying a tray of samples. Normally, a restaurant would hand out samples to potential customers. But this girl was weaving in and out of the picnic tables handing out samples to those of us who were already stuffing our faces with her restaurant's chicken sandwiches!

Lisa said, "Ed, that's hilarious. I mean, all she has to do is walk about fifteen paces, go out to all the hundreds of people who obviously haven't eaten yet, and offer the food to them. Yet, she's content to feed the already fed." And that's when it hit me like an all-pro NFL linebacker. I said, "Lisa, that's it! That is the local church in a nutshell." You see, our problem is that we've been so content weaving in and out of the church aisles and handing out samples to the already fed that we have missed the countless opportunities to offer the food, the very bread of life, to a lost and dying world.[68]

We communicate in a language that feeds the already fed. Instead, we need to communicate in a language that's simple enough to feed

---

[68] Ed Young Jr., "Communicating with Creativity," *Preaching* 20, no. 6 (May-June 2005): 9, 10.

those who need to be fed—those who are not being fed at all. In other words, we spend more time speaking to the converted in a complex language that only they understand, when we should be trying to communicate to the unconverted, in simple language they can understand.

THE KISS PRINCIPLE

It's no wonder that so many people are walking out of churches confused. So what's the solution? I believe it's wrapped up in one word—KISS—*keep it short and simple.* Keep your sentences short and your words simple. Our goal should be to speak in such a way that the most common, everyday person can understand what we're saying. That also makes it easy for everyone else to understand what we're talking about. The majority of daily newspapers across the United States and Canada are written at a grade eight level. Why? Because they want to keep it short and simple so that their readers can understand the stories. Rick Warren reminds us:

> Jesus used simple language. He didn't use technical or theological jargon. He spoke in simple terms that normal people could understand. We need to remember that Jesus did not use the classical Greek language of the scholar. He spoke in Aramaic. He used the street language of that day and talked of birds, flowers, lost coins and other everyday objects that anyone could relate to.
>
> Jesus taught profound truths in simple ways. Today we do the opposite. We teach simple truths in profound ways. Sometimes when pastors think they are being "deep" they are really just being "muddy." Mark 12:27 says, "The common people heard Him gladly." Now if that's the way Jesus preached, that's the way I want to preach. That the common people hear you gladly. Spurgeon said, "A sermon is like a well; if there's anything in it, it appears bright and reflective." But he said, "If there's nothing in it, it appears dark and deep and mysterious." And he said, "There are a lot of deep preachers that are just empty wells with a dead cat or two in them." You know, it's easy to complicate the gospel. It's much more diffi-

cult to be simple. And the simplest things are the strongest things.

When I compare my kids' toys, my little boy has these molded plastic toys that have no moveable parts. You know, you throw them against the wall and they don't break, they're unbreakable. My older boy has these robotronic toys, you know, with all these moveable parts. Which toy do you think breaks easier? The complex one. The simplest is the strongest. That's true in preaching. That's true in outlines. The simplest outline is the strongest outline. Einstein said, "You really don't understand something unless you can say it in a simple way." So I would tell you, don't be afraid of being called a simple teacher or a simple preacher. Wear that as a badge of honor. Take that as a compliment.[69]

Rick adds:

Chuck Swindoll and I—along with Jack Hayford and Chuck Smith—once taught a seminary course on preaching. We each taught how we prepare and deliver sermons. At the end of the course, the students mentioned that all four of us had—without collaboration—emphasized the same thing: *keep it simple!* It's easy to complicate the gospel, and of course, Satan would love for us to do just that.[70]

In communication, even more important than the content is the delivery. A famous study by psychologist Albert Mehrabian shows that almost 40% of our communication is wrapped up in our delivery, how we say what we say.[71] And in television, a lot of emphasis is placed not only on what is said but also on how it's said.

---

[69] Warren, "How to Communicate to Change Lives—Part 2."
[70] Warren, "Preaching for Life Change," 19.
[71] Albert Mehrabian's study shows that 7% of a speaker's message comes from his words—what he says; 38% from his delivery—how he says it; and 55% from his physiology—his bodily movements. Therefore, more than 90% of a speaker's communication is non-verbal.

Jesus Himself placed a lot of importance on how to say it. In John 12:49, He said, "The Father who sent me commanded me *what to say* and *how to say it*" (NIV, italics mine). God was not only concerned with what Jesus said, but also with how He said it. "All over America, baseball pitchers stand the same distance from home plate, throw the same ball, to the same plate. The difference between pros and amateurs is delivery. And the difference between a good sermon and an outstanding sermon is delivery."[72]

Conversationally Speaking

Television speaks a language that viewers understand, and it does it in a conversational manner. A news anchor doesn't begin a newscast with "I have three stories I want to share with you tonight and they all begin with the letter *c*. We're going to talk about the *corruption* in the White House, the *catastrophe* in Florida and the *cold* weather heading our way." If I were watching a newscast that was presented that way, I'd click to another channel before the anchor got to the third *c*. It's a boring way to communicate, so why are we still doing it today?

I love what a successful defense lawyer once said: "If you argue 10 points, even if each is a good point, when they get back to the jury room they won't remember any."[73] And how effective do you think Jesus would have been as a communicator if every time He got up to speak He started with "There are three things I want to show you today" or "Here are four things you need to know"? I doubt very much that the crowds would have "hung on every word he said" (Luke 19:48, NLT) if He communicated that way. Duane Litfin supports this idea:

> Haddon Robinson said the day of the preacher is over; the day of the communicator is here. And that's really what he means. If you're sort of an old-style preacher, the old-fashioned way, if you're going up there with your famous three points and a poem, if your structures sound like "My first point is...my sec-

---

[72] Michael Duduit, "Purpose-Driven Preaching: An Interview with Rick Warren," *Preaching* 17, no. 2 (September-October 2001): 16.
[73] Heath and Heath, *Made to Stick*, 16.

ond point is...the first reason to do so and so is...the second reason...," I'm not saying don't do that. I'm just saying that those structures sound like a preacher talking, and in this generation that is not what people are attuned to. They are driven by the media, and the media does not sound like a preacher talking. It doesn't have that old-fashioned shape and sound and feel to it. And so if you get into your preacher voice and you get into your preacher's structures and preacher approaches, you are just sounding like something from a previous time, and you are not really adapting yourself to your audience.[74]

REPLACE YOUR POINTS WITH MOVES

In a normal conversation, there are small modules of thought throughout. For example, in a short five- to ten-minute conversation, two people might chat about the weather, the rising gas prices, the need for more fuel-efficient cars, and how company mergers and downsizing are a constant threat to the average employee. These modules of thought flow from one to the other. The person starting the conversation doesn't say, "I want to talk to you about the weather, rising gas prices, the need for more fuel-efficient cars and company mergers and downsizing." The conversation just flows that way, moving from one module of thought to the next. In your preaching, you can replace points with modules of thought, which David Buttrick in his book *Homiletic* calls "moves." The whole idea is to steer your communication style away from sounding like a lecture and towards sounding like a conversation. Points, or Roman numerals, become moves, because in the end that's what people hear. A message is still constructed with an outline, but what people hear during that message is a series of moves. So, in essence, your moves are simply mile markers to tell you—and only you—where you are in your message.

---

[74] Duane Litfin, "A Preaching Style for this Generation," *Looking to Jesus*, Preaching Today, cassette no. 178.

Haddon Robinson offers a great example of how to turn your points into moves:

> One thing you can do to use the outline and make it flow is to design the sermon as you would a conversation, so that each of the points, or each of the moves in the sermon, as you think of your Roman numerals, are related to what goes before. What I mean by that is, if you were preaching a sermon on forgiveness, in the introduction you might deal with the need for forgiveness, why you're bringing this up. You might come out of that and move into your first movement in your sermon and say, "Forgiveness is necessary." And then the second move would be, "But even though forgiveness is necessary, we often find it difficult." And then the third move could be, "But there's good news. As difficult as forgiveness might be, we who are Christians can be particularly good at it because we are followers of Jesus Christ." So that when you outline your sermon, the major movements in your sermon can be read out loud like a conversation, rather than just three bare statements. I think that enables you to have an outline, but it doesn't come through like the bones of a skeleton.[75]

In a five- or ten-minute conversation, you can cover three, four or even five different moves. However, during the same time in a message you should only cover one or no more than two moves, because "Nothing forms in people's consciousness unless you work at it for at least three minutes. That is, if you just give something in passing, it will not form in people's consciousness. Nothing happens inside of them."[76] Therefore, each idea needs to be developed for at least three minutes so that people fully grasp what's being said. It's not a coincidence that the average length of a song on the radio is three-and-a half minutes. Record companies purposely produce radio-edit versions of

---

[75] Robinson, "How to Bring Clarity to Sermons."
[76] Robinson, "Preaching in a Television Age."

songs with that length in mind, because they know it's just the right amount of time to drive home the hook of the tune.

STOP THE ALLITERATION!

Alliteration is another ineffective way to communicate. Not only do people not talk that way, but there are also some real dangers in communicating biblical truth that way. Don Sunukjian mentions four worth noting:

Alliteration…

May cause the speaker to use a word nobody knows, and thus to be unclear. To sustain the same alphabet letter, the speaker searches his thesaurus. Unfortunately, the only word that accurately conveys his concept is a word few of his listeners are familiar with.

Runs the danger of changing the biblical author's meaning. If the speaker resolves to alliterate with only familiar words, he may find himself finessing or manipulating the true meaning of the text to remain intelligible to the listener. The speaker may be clear, but now he is biblically inaccurate.

Suggests to the listener that the most important thing to remember in the message is the outline. It subtly says to the listener, "Get this outline! Remember it!" But what the listener really needs to get is the central truth and its relevance for his life. He should walk away from the message not with an outline but with an awareness of how a biblical truth bears on his life. His mind should be engaged not with points but with how he, in some concrete way, is going to think or act differently as a result of his time with God.

May draw the listener's attention more to our cuteness and cleverness than to the truth of God's Word. He may appreciate our skill more than he absorbs God's message.[77]

---

[77] Don Sunukjian, "Four Things That Can Happen When You Alliterate, and Four of Them Are Bad," *Preaching* 16, no. 3 (November-December 2000): 34, 35.

Communicators who use alliteration do so hoping that it will make it easier for their audience to remember their points, but every speaker I have heard use alliteration ends up looking at his notes. So if the communicators can't remember what their alliterated words are, what makes them think that the audience will remember them?

To ensure that the audience will remember your points, instead of giving them three, four or five alliterated ones, just give them one, simply worded, and turn the remaining points into separate messages. This will be discussed fully in Chapter 7.

OHHH GOD...

Another area that cannot be overlooked is the way you come across. In other words, what do you sound like? Do you use a stained-glass, holier-than-thou voice, perhaps trying to imitate what you think God's voice would sound like if you could hear Him? Do your prayers sound something like "Oh God, Thou who art the Maker of the universe, we thank Thee for Thy omniscience, Thy omnipresence and Thy omnipotence. And we thank Thee that we can talk to Thee in prayer"? That's not how I hear people speak at the mall—or anywhere else for that matter. The way common people sound when they speak is the way we need to sound when communicating God's Word.

YOU MAKE ME WANNA SHOUT!

Over one hundred years ago, there weren't any public address systems. There were no microphones, amplifiers, or speakers. And when you had an auditorium filled with a few hundred people, the speaker would have to shout to make himself heard in the back of the room. The problem today is that many preachers haven't realized that's no longer the case. Today, we have microphones that suit every taste. There are handheld mics, lapel mics and mics that come around your cheek and are fixed in front of your mouth. Public address systems today are so advanced that even the people in the back of the room can hear you breathing! Yet some preachers still choose to shout. And that kind of communication style just doesn't connect at all with the people who come to church these days. People in our culture don't want to come to church to be yelled at, and when they are, they're turned off by it and stop coming. Can you imagine David Letterman, Ellen DeGeneres and Larry King speaking continuously at the top of their lungs for an hour during their shows? Would you continue to watch? And what do you think would happen to their studio audiences for the next day's shows? Do you think anyone would show up? I don't think so.

Do you know what's even more of a turn-off? Have you ever noticed the pronoun that the stained-glass-voice guy and the shouter use the most? Their favorite pronoun is *you*. And their messages are filled with a number of imperatives such as "you must" and "you should" and "you have to." If we're going to reach today's people, we have to drop the *you* and replace it with the all-inclusive *we*. When a preacher always says, "You must do this, and you should be doing more of that," it frustrates the listeners to the point where they say, "Who does that guy think he is?" And when that happens, the listeners will either stop coming to church, stop listening to the radio broadcast or stop watching the TV program.

BE YOURSELF

Points, alliteration, a stained-glass voice, shouting and a constant barrage of commands—is it any wonder why this communication style doesn't attract today's audiences? What's the solution? It's wrapped up in two words: be yourself! More than ever before, people today want to know that you're real. Have you ever stopped to wonder why reality TV has become so popular? It exposes people as they really are, and viewers like that. Today more than ever, people want to get to know the real you. The person they see on the platform shouldn't be any different than the person they sit with to have coffee. Andy Stanley agrees:

> Much has been written on the importance of being yourself as a communicator. And I would agree. Authenticity communicates volumes. Authenticity covers a multitude of communication sins. If a communicator is honest and sincere, I can put up with a lot of things. But if I get the feeling that I'm listening to their stage personality, that's a big turnoff. I imagine you are the same way. I want to hear you, not your best rendi-

tion of your favorite communicator. I love what Chuck Swindoll says about this: know who you are, accept who you are and be who you are.[78]

Ed Young Jr. encourages us to:

Study others, but don't copy them. The most important principle for effective communication is to let you be you. Don't imitate another speaker. You can learn some tips and techniques from others, but be the unique person God has made you to be. Just be yourself and improve on the personality and skills that God has given you.[79]

In his book, *My Remarkable Journey*, the incomparable communicator Larry King, who is truly in a league of his own and watched by millions of viewers every night, shares how he was approached by a university years ago and asked if he would like to teach a course on interviewing. He declined the offer because he said that he didn't think he would have anything different to say on the third week than he would on the first. The lesson's the same—just be yourself.

God only made one you, and He will never make anyone else like you. Let your communication style celebrate who *you* are.

---

[78] Stanley and Jones, *Communicating for a Change*, 169.
[79] Young Jr., "Keys to Creative Communication," 13.

Close-Up Shot

- Watch your language.
- Speak in a conversational manner.
- Be yourself.

6

TELEPROMPTING THE TEXT

"You wouldn't go to a play and expect the actors on stage to have cue cards or notes and pause every so often to look at what they needed to say next."

—Don Sunukjian—

A teleprompter is a display device used in television that prompts the person speaking with an electronic visual text. The screen is in front of the lens of the camera, and the words on the screen are reflected to the eyes of the speaker using a one-way mirror. It looks as though the speaker is not using any notes and has memorized everything he or she is saying.

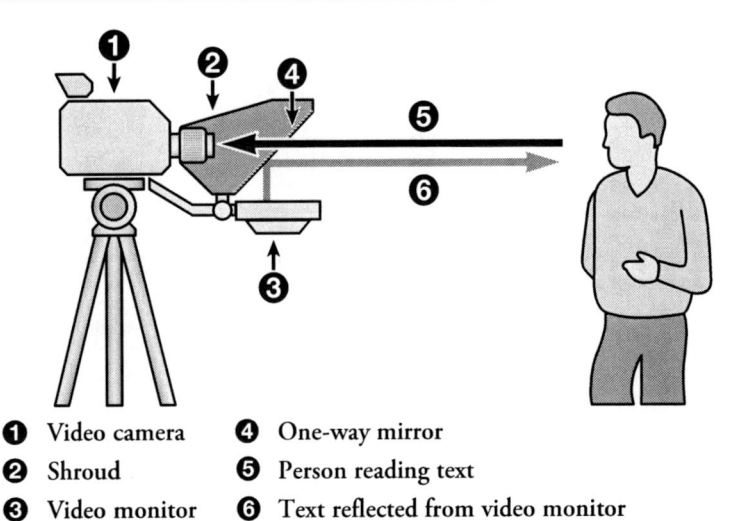

❶ Video camera
❷ Shroud
❸ Video monitor
❹ One-way mirror
❺ Person reading text
❻ Text reflected from video monitor to one-way mirror

If you're interested in taking your communication skills to another level, I recommend that you learn to speak without notes. Andy Stanley says:

> Odds are you want to become more conversational in your communication style. To do that, you can't be tied to your notes. The only people who converse with notes are people auditioning for a part in a play. But even the most amateur actors would never dream of walking out on stage with their script. Why? Because a good actor doesn't want to be caught acting. They want their audience to believe that they really are who they are pretending to be; that they really feel what they're pretending to feel; that the words they say come from their heart, not a script. And we do, too![80]

Manuscript Required

One thing is fundamental to every type of television program, whether it's news, a documentary, sports, a sitcom, drama or entertainment. Each one requires a manuscript. A manuscript brings a show

---

[80] Stanley and Jones, *Communicating for a Change*, 133.

to life. It clearly spells out the beginning from the end and everything in between. In short, television producers can't produce a thing without a manuscript. You could say the manuscript is their bible. And the same is true for movies and theatre productions. I have often heard actors during interviews say that a movie is only as good as its script.

I have met many pastors over the years who don't prepare manuscripts for their messages. Most use an outline of some sort, but many stop at the outline and don't write their messages in full. The outline is extremely important to have because it's the foundation that the manuscript is built upon. But if the outline represents the skeleton of a message, then the manuscript is the flesh that forms the body around that skeleton. Another way to look at it is that your outline is the road map to your destination for a particular message and your manuscript is the physical vehicle that gets you there. The outline and the manuscript work hand in hand. They are both important. You can't have one without the other.

You will not be able to communicate without notes if you don't have notes. Are you just going to say whatever comes to your mind? Or are you depending on the Holy Spirit to give you the words you need to speak when you walk onto the platform? Speakers who do that give the Holy Spirit a bad name because they make Him come across as unprepared and disorganized. If you're going to communicate without notes, you're going to need a manuscript; you're going to have to begin to write your messages out in full.

Can you imagine a news anchor going to air without having written anything? How about a comedian hitting the stage and trying to wing his entire routine? Or an actor in a sitcom who is told by the scriptwriter to "Just make it up as you go along"? How long do you think a show like that would stay on the air? Yet, I know many preachers who show up on Sunday mornings and make it up as they go along. Sitting through a message like that is agonizing. By the end of the message you've counted every ceiling tile and every floor tile in your immediate area and planned how you're going to spend the rest of your Sunday. Preparing a manuscript is foundational, not only in helping you communicate without notes, but also in perfecting the craft of effective communication. And those who fail to prepare one prepare for one thing—failure!

Haddon Robinson says:

> If you are going to come to grips with language there is no way I know you can do it apart from a manuscript. Writing takes the fuzz off your thought. For me, it is not simply a way of putting something into a manuscript, it's a way of thinking; in fact, so much so that I do not know how to think without writing. Even if I have to do a ten-minute devotional, I will write it out. I don't use it in the pulpit, I preach without notes, but I will have written that devotional out in full, simply because there is no way I know that you can really come to grips with language without writing it.[81]

Haddon's son, Torrey, agrees:

> I think it's very important to have a manuscript because, at least for me, it helps me to think through what I'm going to say more clearly. I can think through, for example, not just that I need to have an illustration, but I have to write out the illustration and make sure it's very clear in my mind. I think for clarity purposes and just for finished purposes, the wording and thoughts are clearer when you have to write them down.[82]

Don Sunukjian perhaps said it best: "I think a manuscript brings precision to your wording. If you don't know how you're going to say what you're going to say, it may not come out the best way you want it to come out."[83]

And Chuck Swindoll creatively put it this way:

> Writing makes a man exact. I think: if it doesn't make sense on paper, it's not going to make sense verbally. The discipline of

---

[81] Haddon Robinson, "Biblical Preaching Lecture Series," Tyndale Seminary, 1984.
[82] Personal interview with Torrey Robinson, 26 September 2005.
[83] Personal interview with Don Sunukjian, 10 July 2006.

writing it down will help disentangle your thoughts. I learned a little piece years ago: "Thoughts disentangle themselves through the lips and over the fingertips."[84]

So get into the habit of writing your messages out in full. You will be amazed at how much clearer your messages will be. Duane Litfin says, "There is nothing you can do that will contribute more to improving your speaking style than writing out your entire speech, word for word as you intend to say it."[85]

INTERNALIZE—DON'T MEMORIZE!

Communicating without notes doesn't mean you have to memorize your manuscript. But you will have to internalize your message. Haddon Robinson explains:

> When you preach without notes you don't memorize the sermon. What you do is internalize it. That is, if you have a flow of thought, then you have to be able to remember how that flow goes. The secret of it is in the way you prepare. If you have an outline that is logical or psychological, you'll discover that a good talk remembers itself. The flow is there. Research says that a small number of notes doesn't get in your way, like a small one page, one side, doesn't get in your way, but more than that affects communication, so it's worth a try; it's worth doing it.
>
> Years ago, when I got out of Dallas seminary, I was preaching in San Diego. I'm sure I had an extensive use of notes, but on the way out a sailor said to me, "Preacher, if you can't remember it, how do you expect us to remember it?" That was a great word. And in our day, preaching without notes is not just, you know, "Look, Ma, no hands." It really becomes essential for communication. Watch television, and

---

[84] Michael Duduit, "Preaching and the Holy Spirit: An Interview with Chuck Swindoll," *Preaching* 9, no. 3 (November-December 1993): 22.
[85] Litfin, *Public Speaking*, 304.

they do everything to keep you from thinking that they're even looking at a script. They're always staring at you. Look at good speakers. Look at the political speakers. They don't sit there and read a manuscript. There's a vitality of speech. And so you don't have to remember it all. What you're really doing is, you're internalizing it; you're not trying to memorize it.[86]

Andy Stanley says:

> I find something very disingenuous about the speaker who says, "This is very, very important," and then reads something from his notes. Constantly referring to notes communicates "I have not internalized this message. I want everybody else to internalize it, but I haven't."[87]

When you memorize a manuscript, your focus is on the individual words. But when you internalize a message, your primary focus is on the individual chunks of the outline—the introduction, the individual moves, the application and the conclusion. The key thing is to make sure your outline flows. Make sure it has unity, order and progress, because those are things that the human mind craves. And you accomplish this flow by making sure that the individual moves of your outline are parallel to the moves of your text. Your text becomes your guide, prompting you to remember your next move and what you're going to say about it.

Trying to memorize a speech word for word is very stressful. And you can tell when someone has memorized something, because it sounds robotic. It doesn't flow like a natural conversation. Instead, visualize the individual chunks of the outline and read them through enough times that you're able to deliver them in a conversational style. You internalize a message by visualizing it. Once you're able to visualize the big pieces, or the flow of the outline, you can then focus on the words that make up the manuscript that you prepared for each part.

---

[86] Robinson, "How Can I Speak So An Audience Will Listen?"
[87] Stanley and Jones, *Communicating for a Change*, 135.

Here's how I do it. Once I've completed my manuscript, I start at the beginning and read through it, highlighting in bold the key nouns, verbs, names, places and facts, such as dates, measurements and monetary conversions. The bolded words not only trigger my memory but also help me visualize and internalize the content of that particular chunk of the message. They help seal it in my mind.

An analogy I came across helps to explain this sealing process. Think of your memory as being like Velcro. If you look at the two sides of Velcro material, you'll see that one side is covered with thousands of tiny hooks and the other side is covered with thousands of tiny loops. When you press the two sides together, the hooks get snagged inside the loops, and that's what causes the Velcro to seal. Likewise, your brain hosts a truly staggering number of loops. The more hooks an idea has, the better it will cling to your memory.[88] As I read through my manuscript and bold key words, those words become the loops that hook to my memory, which help seal that particular chunk of the message.

Once I've gone through the message with the individual chunks clearly divided, bolded all the key words within each chunk, and read it through a number of times, I can now visualize it and remember it. Those individual pieces of the message, such as the introduction and the moves, have become big pictures for me, with key words from the manuscript in bold beside them.

Following is the introduction portion of one of my manuscripts, a message on Psalm 73, entitled *Doubting God*, prepared in the way that I read through it to internalize it.

Message Title: Doubting God
Text: Psalm 73

INTRODUCTION:

- The question I have for you today is this: As a **Christian**, as a person who claims to **follow God**, does it bother you when you see **non-**

---

[88] Heath and Heath, *Made to Stick*, 110, 111.

Christians who want nothing to do with **God, Church or the Bible?** Does it bother you to see people like that do really well?
- I'm speaking of the [1] people who are living in the **BIG houses** that are **paid for,** [2] **driving the fancy cars,** [3] have the **six-** or even **seven-digit incomes** and [4] get to go on **two or three trips** a year.
- How does that make you **feel?** Have you ever **questioned God** about that? Have you ever thought, *God, how come they have so much and they don't even know You, and here I am trying to be as faithful as I know how and I'm struggling?*
- Have you ever **gotten angry** with God about that? More **importantly,** have you ever **doubted God** because of that? Have you ever thought, *What's the use? This Christianity stuff doesn't seem to be working. I was better off when I didn't know God.*

BACKGROUND:

- Well, if you've ever spoken words like that, I can tell you that **you're not alone.** In fact, we're going to take a look at a passage in the **Old Testament** today that was written by a man who **felt** the same things you perhaps have felt and **said** the same things you perhaps have said.
- His name is **Asaph. Who is Asaph?** Well, you'll be interested to know that Asaph was a **Levite** who headed the **services of music** during the reigns of **David and Solomon.** In short, Asaph was David and Solomon's **worship leader.** He was the one who led the **people of God** into the **presence of God,** through his **music and praise.** And so we're talking here about a very **important spiritual leader** during the reigns of David and Solomon.
- And what we're going to look at today is one of the **12 psalms** that Asaph wrote. It's **Psalm 73.**
- And if you're **not familiar** with this psalm, you may be **quite surprised** to find out that you and Asaph may have a **few things in common.**

At this point I would read a portion of the text and flow into the first move of the message, which would be broken down with key words bolded in the same manner as the introduction. This essentially creates what we call in television a storyboard, a series of individual pic-

Stop Preaching and Start Communicating

tures that describes a particular scene in a commercial, and beside each picture the script that goes along with that particular shot. As was discussed in Chapter 5, when you replace your points with moves, you're no longer preaching a sermon. Instead, you're conversationally communicating a message in the form of a story. You're speaking to people the way people speak. And the bonus is that because your message flows like a story, it makes it much easier to remember.

The following is a typical television storyboard of a 30-second commercial that will help you visualize this idea. You will first see the script and shot list on one page, which is then followed by the storyboard that provides you with a shot by shot visual of what it will look like on screen.

Tony Gentilucci

Commercial Title: **ROYAL'S GYM**
Scriptwriter: Jeanne Pappas Simon
Commercial Length: 30 seconds

VIDEO:	**AUDIO:**
Medium shot of workout woman.	I don't wear lace. And bows? Definitely not me.
Wide shot of group aerobics.	I do work out though. I like a no-nonsense, pounding, sweat-dripping workout, and I can get that at Royal's Gym.
Quick shots of weights, stationary bikes and people running on an indoor track.	They've got free weights, the hot new bikes, and an awesome indoor padded track.
O.T.S. (Over-the-shoulder) shot, past woman, of monitors on the wall.	Plus, Royal's has walls and walls of monitors playing the latest music videos that keep the place movin'.
Racquetball court with woman playing.	Oh yeah, I almost forgot…they have four racquetball courts.
Close-up shot of woman.	And Mom…I never let the boys win.
Royal's Gym Logo.	Royal's—the place for a serious workout.

Stop Preaching and Start Communicating

Page 1 of 3

Project: Royal's Gym

I don't wear lace.
And bows?
Definitely not me.

I do work out though.
I like a no-nonsense,
pounding, sweat-
dripping workout,

and I can get that at
Royal's Gym.

Boards by Mark Simon 407-370-BORD (2673)
www.storyboards-east.com

Tony Gentilucci

Page 2 of 3

Project: **Royal's Gym**

They've got free weights, the hot new bikes,

and an awesome indoor padded track.

Plus, Royal's has walls and walls of monitors playing the latest music videos that keep the place movin'.

Boards by Mark Simon 407-370-BORD (2673)
www.storyboards-east.com

Stop Preaching and Start Communicating

Project: **Royal's Gym**

Page 3 of 3

Oh yeah, I almost forgot...they have four racquetball courts.

And Mom...I never let the boys win.

Royal's—the place for a serious workout.

Boards by Mark Simon 407-370-BORD (2673)
www.storyboards-east.com

Your Storyboard Is Your Teleprompter

In the Royal's Gym storyboard, the pictures along with the script beside each shot tell the story. In a message outline, the individual chunks—the introduction, moves and the application—become the big pictures of your message, with the manuscript written beside them with key words in bold font. This is what helps you internalize the message. It helps you "associate" the chunks. The completed storyboard, made up of your outline and manuscript, becomes in effect your teleprompter, just like the one they use in television. But this teleprompter is in your mind. In equation form it would look something like this:

[1] Message Outline + Manuscript = Message Storyboard
[2] Message Storyboard = Teleprompter (in your mind)

As you begin a message and the teleprompter in your mind begins to scroll down, you're able to see the chunk you're communicating, and you're prompted to recall your manuscript by visualizing the key words that you bolded throughout that particular chunk. The following is a short sample from the message on Psalm 73 to help you visualize it.

Message Storyboard/Teleprompter
Message Title: Doubting God
Text: Psalm 73

Introduction/ Text Background	The question I have for you today is this: As a **Christian**, as a person who claims to **follow God**, does it bother you when you see **non-Christians** who want nothing to do with **God, Church or the Bible**? Does it bother you to see people like that do really well?...
Move #1 — We doubt God when our circumstances contradict our faith.	The psalm **begins** in a very **interesting manner**. In verse 1, we can clearly see the worship leader in **Asaph** when he proclaims, "**God is good!** God is good to those who are pure in heart!" I mean, so far so good, right?...

...Beginning in verse 4, speaking of those **wicked rich** people, **Asaph** goes through a **shopping list** of things that he has **noticed** about them. He says it seems that:
  i. they live **painless** lives
  ii. their bodies are **healthy** and **strong**
  iii. their lives are **trouble-free**...

> **Move #2**
> But we defeat our doubts about God when we see things the way He sees them.

Verse 17 says that Asaph **enters** the **sanctuary** of God, and I have to say that I find it very interesting that Asaph would **seek** God at a **time** when he was **doubting** Him. Usually we want to do the exact **opposite**. We want to be as **far** as we can from **God** when we're **doubting** Him. Instead, Asaph **drew near** and something happened... **God spoke**...

> **Application**
> Disciplines for regaining God's perspective on life.

Now, **I don't know** how **drawing** near to God in **regaining** His perspective is going to look like for you, but there are certain **disciplines** that all of us can **practice** in order to **regain** God's **perspective** on life. Some of them include...

> **Conclusion**

Are you doubting God today? **Defeat your doubts** about **Him** by **seeing things** the way **He sees** them.

In the end, you haven't memorized a manuscript but internalized a message. And you may not have a physical teleprompter positioned in front of you, but you do have a mental one allowing you to visualize and recall what you need to say.

Talk Out Loud!

You have the outline. You've prepared the manuscript. You've bolded the key words. You're able to clearly visualize the flow of the message from chunk to chunk. And you've read it through several times to internalize it. Now you're thinking *Let's go communicate this baby.* Well, not just yet. There is one last step before the message can be delivered—you need to rehearse it out loud. The key to all mastery is repetition. And repetition in the case of an oral communicator is nothing more than mental push-ups. The more you repeat the material, the stronger the mental links become forged into your memory. And when you take the significant extra step of rehearsing your message out loud, your ability to recall the material skyrockets. Why? Because the words on paper have now come to life by amplifying them with voice and emotion, which produces peak mental fitness and agility. Therefore, repetition via rehearsing the material out loud dramatically increases recall. Repeat. Rehearse. Recall. It's as simple as that.

In the arts world, whether it's television, theater or film, nothing is done without rehearsing. In fact, in theater and television they have full dress rehearsals, because they don't want any surprises to catch them off guard when they're doing it for real in front of a live audience.

Rehearsing your message out loud can make the difference between a good message and a great one. You will approach the platform with confidence instead of second-guessing yourself as you make your way up there. You will feel like a disciplined runner who has trained hard and knows he's going to win the race instead of feeling that you don't stand a chance. In short, this one step will make or break the message. To feel that you really *own* it, you need to rehearse it out loud. You need to hear yourself to know if it flows and if anything is not clear. If you're bumping up against something that is difficult to explain or that you've complicated, it allows you to make the necessary changes to clarify and simplify it.

Where Do You Rehearse?

I rehearse in the car during my daily drive to work. I don't want it to look like I'm talking to myself, so I put the earpiece of my cell phone in my ear so it looks like I'm talking on the phone. I find it's more convenient than trying to find a 30-minute block of uninterrupted time at home or work. Because I have the message chunked and visualized in my mind, if I get to my destination before I finish rehearsing the whole thing, the chunks act as bookmarks for me. When I return to the car, I pick up from the chunk where I left off and continue from there. If I'm working at smoothing out a chunk that has a few bumps in it, I can scroll my mental teleprompter up or down and rehearse out loud that portion of the message.

If you take the time to rehearse your messages out loud, you'll never walk onto any platform again with the slightest bit of anxiety, feeling that you're not ready. The only anxiety you'll feel is the kind that motivates you to get up there and give them everything you've got.

Oops ...

You may be thinking *What if I do all that you suggested and I forget something?* The short answer is that's okay. Relax. Breathe. It will happen from time-to-time. But here are two things to keep in mind: you and you only will know that you missed something. Your audience will never know a thing unless you deliberately make them aware of it, either via your body language, or by saying something about it. I strongly recommend you do neither. The ONLY thing to do when you can't recall something is to keep going. Don't stop. Keep your mental teleprompter moving forward to the next point.

Secondly, in my own experience, I've noticed that anything I've ever forgotten to communicate during a message, which is usually a few sentences of supporting material, was simply TMI (too much information) and I should have left it out to begin with. Plus, it almost always has very little to zero impact on the overall message.

The Benefits

Communicating without notes…

Does not tie you to a pulpit. Because you don't have notes, you no longer have to stand like a statue behind a pulpit with both hands gripping the sides.

Allows you to get physical. Because you no longer have to stand in one position, you can now move around and gesture freely. Over 50% of our communication is in our bodily movements, so let your body talk.

Makes you believable. When you have internalized the message by preparing the manuscript, chunking it like a storyboard in your mind and rehearsing it out loud, you sound believable.

Allows you to gauge audience reaction. You can tell if your audience is tracking with you. Are their eyes fixed on you, or are they playing Eye Spy? Are their bodies still and silent or moving restlessly in their seats? Do they lean slightly forward, communicating that they don't want to miss a word you're saying? Or are they slouched back as though they're sitting in recliner chairs?

Allows you to maintain continuous eye contact. By far the biggest advantage of communicating without notes is the fact that you can maintain constant eye contact with the audience. In fact, all of the other advantages mentioned hinge on having uninterrupted eye contact. It establishes instant rapport, keeps the communication open, allows you to express emotion and keeps your audience interested. As well, you won't be bobbing your head up and down between your notes and the audience, which is not only distracting but also unappealing.

A pastor who was at his very first church said to his congregation on his very first Sunday, "Now I'm in the process of learning all this stuff about preaching, so I want you to be real honest and up front with me about how I can improve."

After the service a gentleman walked up to him and said, "Pastor, I want you to know that your sermon wasn't very good."

The pastor, in a transparent manner, responded by saying, "Okay, can you tell me specifically what was wrong with it?"

And the gentleman said, "Well, there were three things wrong with your sermon. Number 1, you read it. Number 2, you read it poorly. And number 3, it wasn't worth reading in the first place."

I am absolutely convinced that communicating without notes will dramatically improve the effectiveness of any communicator.

Close-Up Shot

- To communicate without notes, you need to prepare a complete manuscript.
- Internalize the message—don't memorize the manuscript.
- The biggest benefit of communicating without notes is being able to maintain continuous eye contact with your audience.

7

What's the Point?

"If a message does not have a single point, then the preacher does not have a single sermon, but three or four sermonettes."

—Fred Craddock—

There is one communication principle that television never violates, whether it's an hour-long documentary, a half-hour sitcom, a single news story or a 30-second commercial—one single idea governs whatever is produced. Those who work in television know that people can't handle more than one main idea at a time. That's why they always build their shows around one big idea. In fact, that's how I was trained. Whether it was in my broadcast journalism writing classes or my advertising classes, the instruction was always the same—pick one central idea to govern the entire script.

Then, I went to seminary, where I was introduced to the world of outlines, Roman numerals and multiple points, all foreign to a media guy like me. I had to unlearn all that I had learned during my years of study in that field. And I found the same communication model being practiced at church. I would walk out of church on Sundays with a notepad full of points. So I started to do the same thing. I figured that's just the way it's done in the Church world. They all communicated with a bunch of nicely alliterated points, so I decided to copy that style.

That was until I read *Biblical Preaching* by Haddon Robinson. In the chapter entitled "What's the Big Idea?" Haddon dispelled the notion that the multiple-point model should be the standard in the Church world. He said:

> A sermon should be a bullet, not buckshot. Ideally, each sermon is the explanation, interpretation or application of a single dominant idea supported by other ideas, all drawn from one passage.[89]

Basically, Haddon's book showed me how to incorporate the one big idea message, which I had learned in studying how to write for radio and television, when communicating biblical messages. I immediately dropped the multiple-point model and went back to the way I was originally taught, which I knew in my heart to be much more listener-friendly. I completely agree with Bryan Chapell, who says that "it's easier to catch a baseball than a hand full of sand, even though the two weigh about the same." I decided I no longer wanted to throw sand at people, but rather a baseball they could catch, hold on to and keep as a souvenir. Therefore, this chapter is all about how to search and find the one big idea of a passage, ensuring that the main point is memorable and ringing all of the other subpoints around it. In short, it's all about the power of one–one message, taken from one text, with one main idea.

WHY ONE POINT?

Andy Stanley, who strongly supports the one-point message, has this to say about the multiple-point approach:

> A problem with this [multiple point] approach is that by the time you get to your last point, nobody remembers the first three [assuming there were four points to the sermon]. Whatever impact they might have made is washed away by the information and illustrations that follow. On a good day, it is that last point that usually sticks. And that's assuming it was stated in a way that made it memorable.

---

[89] Robinson, *Biblical Preaching*, 35.

The other problem with preaching points is that it doesn't reflect the world we live in. We don't live our lives by points. We live by our emotions. We respond to what we see, taste and feel. So there's no compelling reason to remember a list of points. They never come in handy. For anything. Even the preacher giving the points knows this. That's why he or she has to refer to their notes. They haven't even bothered to memorize their own points. How ironic. Our points flow from our notes to the listeners' notebooks, assuming they bothered to bring them. In most cases, our *allusive, alluring, alliterated* points move from our notes to our lips into thin air and then back into our files. Seems a bit pointless.[90]

Your one-point messages will have more impact on your audience than any multiple-point message you will ever share with them. Suppose you have two or even four things you want your audience to know. You now have a two- or four-part series. I'll clarify how to deal with subpoints later in this chapter.

THE HOOK

The following is a list of ten of the most popular songs from the last fifty-plus years.

- "Born in the USA"—Bruce Springsteen
- "Celebrate"—Kool and The Gang
- "Hound Dog"—Elvis Presley
- "I Want to Hold Your Hand"—The Beatles
- "I Will Always Love You"—Whitney Houston
- "Satisfaction"—The Rolling Stones
- "Stayin' Alive"—The Bee Gees
- "We Are The Champions"—Queen
- "We Are The World"—Michael Jackson and Lionel Richie
- "YMCA"—The Village People

---

[90] Stanley and Jones, *Communicating for a Change*, 102.

What makes these songs so memorable? I think you would agree that it's the hook of each song. In fact, the hooks have turned some of these songs into anthems of our culture. Record producers work to make the hook of a song as toe-tapping and catchy as they can. And that's the way I want you to think of the one-point message. Think of your one main idea as if it were the hook of a song. Have you ever noticed what record producers do with a hook to make it stand out? They keep it:

- short;
- simple;
- memorable; and they
- repeat it often.

Why One Text?

Biblical literacy among laypeople today is at an all-time low. Few people know their Bibles well enough that you can play biblical hopscotch without confusing them. Because we have some kind of seminary education, we may expect people to be where we are in their knowledge of the Bible, making them feel inadequate. Most of the time that simply comes across as "Look how well I know my Bible."

The ROS Message

ROS is a television term that means "run of schedule." When an advertiser doesn't have enough money to buy a targeted campaign aimed to run in specific programs, they'll buy a ROS package and their commercial will air wherever the station has commercial airtime to fill. The commercial could run at 5:00 in the morning, 2:00 in the afternoon or 11:30 at night. Wherever the station has commercial holes to fill, that's where they'll air the spot. So it's kind of a shotgun, mixed-bag approach to advertising. The advertiser doesn't know where his commercial is going to fall—just that it will air somewhere within the 24-hour broadcast day.

This is quite different from a very targeted rifle approach to advertising, where the commercial is run during specific key programs that deliver large viewing audiences targeted to a particular demographic. How well do you think ROS campaigns work? If you said not very well, you're right. In fact, advertisers frequently cancel ROS campaigns soon after they begin.

Have you ever visited a church where the communicator begins his message, reads the main text and then never refers to or makes comments about that passage again? It's because he's too busy jumping around to other texts. I call it the ROS message, short for "run of Scripture." The person who delivers the ROS message will hop from Old Testament to New, from narrative literature to poetry, from Revelation to Zephaniah, and in the end the audience will get nothing out of the message except confusion.

A ROS Easter Message

Not long ago, I sat through an Easter message where the church had standing room only. Those are great occasions to make an impact on seekers who may be attending church for the very first time. The pastor read the text for the day, 1 Corinthians 15:3-8 and 12-27, but not only did he not take the time to give any kind of background on the passage, he also never made another mention of it. He was too busy hopping around from text to text to text. I lost count of how many other passages he made reference to, so I ordered the DVD and watched the entire sermon again. He actually read from 17 other passages. To confuse the matter even more, he quoted a number of other sources, including a magazine article, a newspaper article, the Christian Science textbook *Science and Health*, an Indian sect called Act Media, an Australian professor at Sydney University, a professor of Oriental law at the University of London, John Calvin's Institutes and the Apostles' Creed. Do you want to know how I walked away that morning? Confused. I didn't understand a thing the guy said, and neither did my wife. Now, if I walked away confused, can you imagine how people who attended that church for the first time must have felt after hearing a smorgasbord of a message like that?

> I can't stand sermons with four and five and six passages. I just think, give me one good one, that's all I need. I want to know what one means. Don't tell me what you want to say and then

give me twelve supporting texts.... I mean, it's real easy to do that, but I don't think it's the best way.[91]

Listen, if you want to do your audience a favor, introduce them to one text. Give your audience a proper background for that particular text, so they can clearly understand and follow what you're saying. And finally, make sure that everything you say throughout the message relates to that one passage, and your audience will love you for it.

Sticking to one text also makes for better Bible interpretation. I don't know how many times I've heard a speaker going from text to text to text to try to prove what he was saying. For example, if he was in James talking about faith, he would add what Hebrews says about faith and then jump to Paul and see what he has to say about faith. If you're in James talking about what James says about faith, stay in James. Haddon Robinson tells us why this is so important:

> The letters were circulated individually, one at a time. They didn't have a whole library of letters that they read over and defined it. It's very dangerous to interpret a passage by looking at four other passages.... To define the writings of Paul by what John says can be very dangerous, with the assumption that they are using the terms in the same way, which is not a valid assumption. It's within the context of the writer, his book, or even his books that you find the best kind of information.[92]

SEARCH AND FIND

Let's look at how to search and find the one main idea of a passage. A lot of the material in this particular section is taken from Haddon Robinson's book *Biblical Preaching*.

To be able to find the main idea of a text, we first need to define what an idea is. According to Haddon, when reduced to its basic structure, an idea consists of only two essential elements: a subject and a

---

[91] Personal interview with Andy Stanley.
[92] Robinson, "Biblical Preaching Lecture Series."

complement. And both are necessary in forming an idea. When Haddon talks about the subject of an idea, he means the complete, definite answer to the question *What is the biblical author talking about?* A subject, therefore, is always worded as a question—who, what, where, when, why or how. And a subject can never be a single word; nor can it stand alone. A subject needs a complement to complete it. The complement completes the subject by answering the question *What is the author saying about what he's talking about?*[93] It should be noted that a subject can have more than one complement.

Haddon clarifies this idea: "If the words *subject* and *complement* confuse you, then try thinking of the subject as a question and your complement as the answer to that question. The two together make up the idea."[94] To further simplify it and help you visualize it in equation form, the formation of an idea based on Haddon's model would be:

Subject (Question: What is the author talking about?)

+   *Complement* (Answer: What is the author saying about what he's talking about?)

=   *The Formation of an Idea*

In essence, this exercise of finding the subject and complement allows you to get to the core idea of the passage, which is exactly what you want.

Once you have the subject and the complement, the two are combined and an idea is shaped. The interrogative is sliced off and an indicative statement is formed, which is called the exegetical idea.[95] But you need to turn the exegetical idea into a homiletical one by using terms that people today can relate to. In other words, you need to state the exegetical idea in 21st-century English. It's simply the biblical truth applied to life. This homiletical idea has been described as a pithy statement of the exegetical idea—brief, forceful and mean-

---

[93] Robinson, *Biblical Preaching*, 41.
[94] Ibid.
[95] Willhite and Gibson (eds.). *The Big Idea of Biblical Preaching*, 166.

ingful in expression; full of vigor and substance. This pithy statement remains faithful to the intention of the text by capturing the idea in a way that listeners will understand.[96] This description perfectly mirrors Haddon's definition of the homiletical idea as "the statement of a biblical concept in such a way that it accurately reflects the Bible and meaningfully relates to the audience."[97] In short, your homiletical idea becomes your one main point, your central idea, your take-home truth, your message slogan, your big idea—the one thing you end up communicating. Ultimately, it's the tagline you want your audience to hear.

Let's look at some examples that highlight one text, its subject, complement, exegetical idea derived from the subject and complement and finally the homiletical idea or the one main point, which is the exegetical idea written for today's audience.

Example #1

Text: Genesis 3:1-6—Satan Tempts Adam and Eve
Subject: How does Satan tempt us?
Complement: He comes to us in disguise and he levels his attack against God.
Exegetical Idea: Satan tempts us when he comes to us in disguise and he levels his attack against God.
Homiletical Idea: Satan disguises himself to cause us to distrust God's character and doubt His Word.[98]

Example #2

Text: Proverbs 11:23-28
Subject: What is the righteous person characterized by?
Complement: He is characterized by good motives that are demonstrated by generosity and trust in the God who cares for him.
Exegetical Idea: The righteous person is characterized by good motives that are demonstrated by generosity and trust in the God who cares for him.

---

[96] Ibid.
[97] Robinson, *Biblical Preaching*, 113.
[98] Willhite and Gibson (eds.). *The Big Idea of Biblical Preaching*, 165, 166.

Homiletical Idea: Changed people spare the change because the God we trust wants us to be generous.[99]

Example #3

Text: Luke 10:25-37—The Parable of the Good Samaritan
Subject: Who is your neighbor?
Complement: He is anyone who I see has a need that I'm able to meet.
Exegetical Idea: My neighbor is anyone I see who has a need that I'm able to meet.
Homiletical Idea: Your neighbor is anyone whose need you see, whose need you're able to meet.[100]

Example #4

Text: Romans 6:1-14
Subject: What happens to the power of sin when a person becomes a Christian?
Complement: Christians die to the rule of sin and are alive to holiness.
Exegetical Idea: Through their union with Jesus Christ in His death and resurrection, Christians have died to the rule of sin and are alive to holiness.
Homiletical Idea: You are not the person you used to be, so don't handle life the way you used to.[101]

Example #5

Text: Psalm 90
Subject: Why are we to count our days?
Complement: So that we may become wiser.
Exegetical Idea: We are to count our days so that we may become wiser in how we live our lives.
Homiletical Idea: Count your days, to make your days count.

---

[99] Haddon Robinson, Scott Gibson, and Jeffrey Arthurs, "The Big Idea of the Sermon," *Pulpit Talk CD* 4, no. 3 (Spring 2006).
[100] Robinson, *Biblical Preaching*, 105.
[101] Ibid.

I completely agree with what J. H. Jowett said about having one central truth govern the entire message:

> I have a conviction that no sermon is ready for preaching, not ready for writing out, until we can express its theme in a short, pregnant sentence as clear as crystal. I find the getting of that sentence is the hardest, the most exacting, and the most fruitful labor in my study. To compel oneself to fashion that sentence, to dismiss every word that is vague, ragged, ambiguous, to think oneself through to a form of words which defines the theme with scrupulous exactness—this is surely one of the most vital and essential factors in the making of a sermon: and I do not think any sermon ought to be preached or even written until that sentence has emerged, clear and lucid as a cloudless moon.[102]

WHAT IF...

What if an idea for a message comes to me before I go to the text? It's happened to me more than once. And those ideas come as we live life. We may notice something while we're driving. We may see something on TV, hear something on the radio, read something on the Internet or in a newspaper or witness something while walking through a shopping mall. An idea can come at any time, anywhere, and when it does, welcome it. But after you've welcomed it, you're going to have to do some digging to find out what the Bible says about your great idea. Here are some questions you should ask:

- What, if anything, does the Bible say about this idea?
- Did anyone in Scripture experience the idea or concept you're thinking of?
- If so, what did or didn't they do in that situation?
- Did Jesus ever address your idea directly or indirectly?[103]

---

[102] Ibid., 37.
[103] Stanley and Jones, *Communicating for a Change*, 107.

"Once you discover a text or a narrative that addresses your *great idea*, let the Bible speak."[104] You need to put the text in the driver's seat and let *it*, not your great idea, drive the message, or you will be communicating your word instead of God's. And if that happens, you're in trouble. Haddon Robinson reminds us:

> While biblical ideas must be shaped to human experience, men and women must be called to conform to biblical truth. "Relevant" sermons may become pulpit trifles unless they relate the current situation to the eternal Word of God.[105]

RING AROUND THE POINT

It's critically important to make sure that all of the subpoints complement the main idea, so that the entire message is focused on that one point. Try picturing the main idea as the hub of a wheel and the subpoints as the spokes, all connected to that one hub. I have delivered messages that contained three or four unrelated points, so in the end I communicated three or four different messages, rather than just one. Now you might be thinking *Well, what's wrong with that? They got more than they came for, right?* The truth is they got less than what they came for, because they all left confused, trying to figure out how what I said all related.

As mentioned earlier, a subject can have more than one complement, and we're to replace our points with moves to embrace a more conversational communication style. Here's how the two are related: your complements are your moves. In other words, the complements that complete your main point represent the moves in your message.

> The move pattern of a message is the coherent development and elaboration of the message statement.... Buttrick uses the term "move" to describe what others call the body or points of the speech or message. Whether this step is called the body, points, main ideas, or major and minor premises, it includes

---

[104] Ibid.
[105] Robinson, *Biblical Preaching*, 30.

two to four major concepts, shifts in direction, or points that are linked coherently to the message statement.[106]

This discipline foolproofs your message, so that all of the subpoints are related to the main idea. The following are the two movements that make up the message for Psalm 73 illustrated in Chapter 6:

Move #1: We doubt God when our circumstances contradict our faith (Psalm 73:1-16).

Move #2: But we defeat our doubts about God when we see things the way He sees them (Psalm 73:17-28).

Big Idea: Defeat your doubts about God by seeing things the way He sees them.

Notice how the two movements above flow from one to the other in a conversational manner and how the second move embraces the big idea. In short, everything is related. All the spokes are connected to the one hub. Donald G. Miller beautifully summarizes this idea:

> Any single sermon should have just one major idea. The points or subdivisions should be parts of this one grand thought. Just as bites of any particular food are all parts of the whole, cut into sizes that are both palatable and digestible, so the points of a sermon should be smaller sections of the one theme, broken into tinier fragments, so that the mind may grasp them and life assimilate them.[107]

Calvin Miller writes:

> The older three-point sermon style should be abandoned in this hard-hitting day of single-emphasis communication. This is not to say, however, that the sermon outline might not have several piers that support this single argument. It's just that these points of supporting logic should not be allowed to

---

[106] Duffet, *A Relevant Word*, 107.
[107] Robinson, *Biblical Preaching*, 36.

develop various separate themes. They should all contribute to building a single emphasis, which the sermon develops from the lone theme it champions.[108]

MAKE IT MEMORABLE

Here are ten different taglines taken from ten different TV commercials. On the right-hand side are the companies those taglines represent. Your task is to match the company to its tagline by writing the letter next to the company name in the blank space provided beside the tagline.

1. Don't leave home without it. _____   A. General Electric

2. Just do it. _____   B. Timex

3. Melts in your mouth,   C. Maxwell House coffee
   not in your hands. _____

4. Takes a licking   D. Rolaids
   and keeps on ticking. _____

5. Reach out and touch someone. _____   E. Kentucky Fried Chicken

6. We bring good things to life. _____   F. American Express

7. Good to the last drop. _____   G. Nike

8. You're in good hands with… _____   M. M & M Candies

9. Finger-lickin' good. _____   I. AT&T

10. How do you spell relief? _____   J. Allstate (Insurance)

(see answers in Appendix 1)

So how did you do? I have no doubt that you did well. This illustrates the power of one idea. The tagline for Maxwell House coffee, "Good to the last drop," has been around since 1926. That was likely before you were even born; yet you were able to recall it instantly.

---

[108] Calvin Miller, *Marketplace Preaching: How to Return the Sermon to Where it Belongs* (Grand Rapids, MI: Baker Books, 1995), 146.

Why? Because the company did two things that were very effective: they made the wording as memorable as possible, and they repeated it in every single commercial. Every commercial ended with the words "Maxwell House coffee...good to the last drop." Concluding all of their commercials consistently with the same tagline worked beautifully in having people instantly recall it every time they heard *Maxwell House coffee*. That's the key behind all one-point messages. If you want your audience to remember your message, the one main idea has to be worded in the most memorable way possible and repeated as often as possible. And who knows? That one point may be remembered years from now.

Here are a few things to keep in mind when crafting a memorable main point—one that's contagious, one that will stick with your audience and not simply go in one ear and out the other.

Keep it short and simple. The KISS principle discussed in Chapter 5 also applies here. When crafting your main point, strive to use one-syllable words in a phrase that has no more than 10 words, and the fewer words the better. The more you reduce the amount of information in an idea, the better it will stick. What you're after is a proverb-type phrase. Proverbs are simple, yet profound; a "short sentence drawn from long experience…. [And] great simple ideas have an elegance and a utility that make them function a lot like proverbs."[109] It does not mean dumbing down, but creating ideas that take the core of the idea, made up of the subject and complement, and making that core idea compact. You're left with a core statement that's compact—meaningful, yet short, simple and sticky. The Golden Rule, "Do for others what you would like them to do for you," is the ultimate model of simplicity. That one phrase is so profound that it can influence a lifetime of behavior. It's a great example of a core idea that is meaningful enough to make a difference in someone's life and also compact enough to be sticky. It's amazing that such a short and simple statement was even given a special name and is known all over the world. It's power-

---

[109] Heath and Heath, *Made to Stick*, 47, 48.

ful, because core and compact statements stick! If you were to just follow this one principle, you would end up producing some very memorable big ideas. You're after a substance-filled, short, sticky statement.

Make each word count. Be ruthless in the editing process of your main point. Cut out every excess word. If you can do without a word, don't use it. Refer to the headlines in newspapers and magazines and notice how they're able to tell you the whole story with very few words. Remember, less is more. And more importantly, less is easier to remember.

State your idea for the ear. You don't have to work at remembering the hook of your favorite songs, and your audience should not have to work at remembering your big idea. They should be able to recall it instantly when heard only once.

Use common everyday words. Study the slogans you see on billboards and in magazine and newspaper ads. Notice their choice of words. Haddon Robinson challenges us with this thought: "If you were given one sentence in which to communicate your idea to someone who didn't know religious jargon and who couldn't write it down, how would you say it?"[110]

Use concrete words. Whatever you do, stay away from abstract words, especially when crafting your main idea. Use a universal language that everyone speaks fluently, made up of concrete words that represent things people can see, touch and feel.

Use positive words. I doubt very much that people will remember a main point full of negative words. Instead, use fresh active words that cut sharply, register quickly and are easily grasped by the listener.

Repeat it often. This is critical. Your main idea should be repeated no less than three times throughout your message, but strive for five or six. The more you repeat it, the better the chances that they'll remember it. That one idea literally becomes your message. If your audience forgets everything else you say and remembers only your main point, you've

---

[110] Robinson, *Biblical Preaching*, 106.

done your job. That's the kind of importance you should place on your main idea when crafting it.

If you follow these seven criteria, you should have a sticky statement, an idea that's useful and long-lasting that will make your audience:

- pay attention;
- understand and remember it;
- agree and believe it;
- care about it; and
- be able to act on it.[111]

> Andy Stanley says:
>
> People are impacted by statements that stick. You need a sticky statement. Take the time to reduce your one point to one sticky statement. It doesn't need to be cute. It doesn't have to rhyme. But it should be short and memorable. Your statement is your anchor. It is what holds the message together and keeps it from drifting off course. This will be what people remember.[112]

Andy's sticky statements that have stuck with me include:

- Our bodies were made by God, for God, to honor God.
- Good people don't go to heaven; forgiven people do.
- When you see as God sees, you will do as God says.

WHAT'S YOUR BURDEN?

What's the one thing that you just have to let your audience know? What is it that's sitting heavy on your heart that you can't wait to communicate? Whatever that one thing is, that's your burden. Your burden is your main idea. And it also fuels the passion for your message. Haddon Robinson reminds us:

---

[111] Heath and Heath, *Made to Stick*, 246.
[112] Stanley and Jones, *Communicating for a Change*, 111.

A novice may dismiss the importance of a central idea as the ploy of homiletics professors determined to press young preachers into their mold. It should be noted, therefore, that the basic fact of communication also claims sturdy biblical support. In the Old Testament, the sermons of the prophets are called "the burden of the Lord." These proclamations were not a few "appropriate remarks" delivered because the prophet was expected to say something. Instead, the prophet addressed his countrymen because he had something to say. He preached a message, complete and entire, to persuade his hearers to return to God. As a result, the sermons of the prophets possessed both form and purpose. Each embodied a single theme directed toward a particular audience in order to elicit a specific response.[113]

Andy Stanley says:

> That one message, idea, principle or truth that had to be delivered…isn't just information. It is not just a carefully crafted phrase. It is literally a burden. It is a burden that weighs so heavily on the heart of the communicator that he or she must deliver it…you can tell when a communicator is carrying a burden versus when he is simply dispensing information.
>
> At some point in the preparation process, you must stop and ask yourself *What is the one thing I must communicate? What is it that people have to know?* If you don't have an answer to that question, you aren't ready. Think about it. If after all your preparation you can't answer that question, what's the point in preaching? If **you** don't know what it is you are dying to communicate, the audience certainly isn't going to be able to figure it out.
>
> Is there anything you are so excited about sharing that you can't wait until you get to that part of the message? If not, you aren't ready. You don't have a burden. You may have pages of information and it may be all true, but if you don't have some-

---

[113] Robinson, *Biblical Preaching*, 37, 38.

thing that people need so badly that you feel compelled to share it, you still have work to do.

The sermons that have put you to sleep were delivered by men with information but no burden. A burden brings passion to preaching. It transforms lifeless theology into compelling truth.[114]

Haddon Robinson says, "A mist in the pulpit is a fog in the pew." In other words, if you don't know what you're talking about, you can rest assured that your audience won't have a clue either. But if you're interested in communicating clear messages that keep people coming back for more every Sunday, then it all comes down to the power of one—communicating one message, taken from one text, with one main idea.

---

[114] Stanley and Jones, *Communicating for a Change*, 113, 114.

Close-Up Shot

- 📹 Search and find the one main idea of a text.
- 📹 Make that one idea memorable.
- 📹 Ring all of the subpoints around that one main idea.
- 📹 Remember, it's all about the power of one. One message, taken from one text, with one main idea.

8

TRICKS OF THE TRADE

"'Winging it' doesn't fly with a TV audience. We do well to set high standards of excellence for ourselves whenever we stand up to speak."

—David Henderson—

Instant replay, teaser, pitch ahead, cross promo, still frame, fast forward—television is full of tricks to keep you watching, and they take advantage of every single one of them so that you won't switch channels. The goal of this chapter is to not only introduce you to some TV lingo but also make you aware of some of the tricks of the TV trade and how you can apply them to your communication style to keep people listening. You'll become more alert in looking out for them when watching television and more intentional in using them when preparing a message. In essence, this chapter is a glossary of television terms arranged in alphabetical order.

CROSS PROMO

Short for cross promotion, it's very similar to the teaser that will be discussed later in this chapter. Basically, a cross promo does exactly what it says—cross promotes one show during another. It's very common for networks to cross promote during their morning program a special that will run in prime time. For instance, during the NBC *Today* morning show, which airs daily between 7:00 a.m. and 10:00 a.m., they will often run a 30-second cross promo or show a clip of an interview that will run during their *Dateline* program that airs at 9:00 p.m. on Thursday nights. Then, at the end of the interview clip, the host will come back on and say something like "Be sure to catch the full story..." or "Be sure to watch the full interview this Thursday night at 9:00 p.m. on *Dateline*, only on NBC."

How can you use cross promotion in your church? You're likely already doing it, but I hope you'll start doing it much more intentionally and strategically. For example, if your youth or missions group is planning something, use the Sunday morning platform to tell people about it; in short, cross promote what one group in the church is doing through another. One church had a missions group going to South America to deliver new bikes to pastors who didn't have anything to get around with, so the person leading the group came into the sanctuary riding a bike and parked it on the platform to show and tell people how their donation dollars had been spent, what the group was doing, why they were doing it and when they were scheduled to leave.

When you cross promote, you're basically sending out the message that the church is alive and active.

Edit

You'll hear this word repeatedly throughout the course of a day at any television station, and it can be defined as cutting the excess or getting rid of what you don't need. Whether it's a television documentary, sitcom or news story, it tries to say everything it needs to say, and no more, in the least amount of time. Television really does believe that less is more.

No one has ever complained to me that I ended a message sooner than they were expecting. And after delivering a message, I have never regretted having edited out certain portions while I was preparing it. Less is more is a line that we hear often, but the question is *Do we practice it?* "Studies show that in our culture, if you preach over 30 to 35 minutes, for every minute or so that you go over you decrease your effectiveness."[115]

---

[115] Haddon Robinson, "Biblical Preaching Lecture Series."

This [editing] can be a frustrating process. If you have spent three or four hours dissecting four or five juicy nuggets from a text, you feel like you need to share 'em all! What a waste to leave so much good stuff on the cutting room floor. But that's exactly what you must discipline yourself to do. Cutting away the peripheral is like narrowing a channel of water. You end up with a much more focused and powerful message people are able to follow, tracking with you as you lead them along. And all that extra stuff? Save it. Sunday comes around every week.[116]

When in doubt take it out. Leave the best and delete the rest. Edit, edit, edit! Trust me, you won't regret it, because less really is more.

EVALUATION

Television is constantly evaluating itself. In fact, a program lives or dies by its ratings. As mentioned in Chapter 4, network executives decide whether to keep a program on the air based on whether or not it's meeting its ratings targets. And a program's ratings are made available to the network literally within hours after the show airs. If people aren't watching it, advertisers aren't buying it, which means the show isn't making money, so it no longer remains on the air. It's as simple as that.

In Chapter 3, I mentioned the significant role that focus groups play in evaluating a program. This is all to say that television goes to great lengths to evaluate how their program line-up is doing. They're very interested in knowing which programs are working and which aren't. And whatever is not working is fixed right away. But if it can't be fixed, they get rid of it.

If you're interested in becoming a better communicator, you're going to need to put some type of evaluation process in place that tells you what you're doing effectively and what you're not. And there are really only two ways to do it. One is evaluating yourself, and the other is having others evaluate you. To evaluate yourself, I suggest listening to your message or, if you have access to video equipment, watching

---

[116] Stanley and Jones, *Communicating for a Change*, 110.

yourself after every message. There may be facial expressions, hand gestures or posture problems you're not aware of that may be distracting or even a complete turn-off for some people. And when you notice those things visually, you can make a conscious effort to correct them. This evaluation idea will not work unless it's done consistently. Then you will be able to tweak little things here and there, which will translate into a big difference, not only for you, but also for your audience.

Bill Hybels, who is a strong advocate of evaluation by others and has been doing it for more than 30 years, says:

> I think probably the best way for a preacher to improve his preaching is to find some very discerning people, godly people in the church, who by invitation of the teacher will lovingly, but truthfully, evaluate each and every sermon and evaluate it in written form and give a written evaluation of it shortly after the message is delivered for the purpose of stimulating that spiritual gift, challenging it to grow, developing it and cheering it on.[117]

Andy Stanley says:

> Every Monday we have an evaluation meeting. I mean, we evaluate ridiculously...music, worship, first service was better than the third. I always have to start the sermon evaluation because they won't. They're sensitive, which I appreciate, but I'm the one that goes in and says, "Okay, first service, B-minus. Second service I felt was an A. Third service, I wish I'd never, you know...." And so, the only way to get better is to evaluate, and I am very quick to put the sermon on the table and say, "You know, we can't go back and redo it, but don't let me make the same mistake twice...." So you know, evaluation is huge. And I listen to almost every message I do; sometimes I listen to [the] first, second and third service, because it's the only way to get

---

[117] Michael Duduit, "A Preaching Interview with Bill Hybels," *Preaching* 7, no. 4 (January-February 1992): 8.

better. And you know, you don't make the same mistake twice. When you hear yourself do it, you fix it quick.[118]

If you're really serious about becoming a better communicator, you'll start evaluating yourself and seeking the constructive comments of others as well.

Fast-Forward

There are times when television deliberately uses a fast-forward technique to get the viewers' attention. To make sure that viewers don't ignore the point they're trying to make, they will hurl an onslaught of images at them in fast-forward. The same can and should be done when you're trying to get a point across. Let's say, for example, you just finished defining sin as missing the mark or, how I like to say it, missing the bull's-eye. To drive that image home, list a series of examples in quick succession:

- God doesn't want us to lie; when we do, we miss the bull's-eye, and that's called sin.
- God doesn't want us to steal; when we do, we miss the mark, and that's called sin.
- God doesn't want us to be unfaithful to our spouses; when we are, we miss the bull's-eye, and that's called sin.
- God doesn't want us acting ugly towards other people; when we do, we miss the mark, and that's called sin.

This fast-forward technique not only helps keep the listeners' attention, but also gives them a number of examples to reinforce the point you're trying to make.

Instant Replay

What would television be without the instant replay allowing you to watch a touchdown, goal or particular play from several different angles? The same principle applies in spoken communication, and we

---

[118] Personal interview with Andy Stanley.

call it restatement. Restatement is different from repetition. "Repetition says the same thing in the same words; restatement says the same thing in different words."[119] And it's very important for us to use both during our messages because we need to always remember that sermons are for listeners, not readers. We write for the ears, not the eyes. The term television uses for repetition is *playback*, which we'll discuss later. But *restatement* is much closer to what television would call the instant replay.

The beauty of the instant replay is being able to see a play from several different angles to appreciate it more fully. And the same holds true when you restate something in different words. People understand more clearly what you're trying to say. It also says to them, "Hey, this is important; you need to get it." And the chance of them getting it is very high because that one point has been impressed in their minds in different ways by using different words.

NARRATIVE COMMUNICATION

Television is a narrative medium. Everything about television is based around a story; even a "news story" tells you the story of a particular incident from beginning to end. Rick Warren states:

> There are many benefits to using stories to communicate spiritual truth: *Stories hold our attention.* The reason television is so popular is because it's essentially a story-telling device, whether you're watching comedy, drama, the news or a talk show. Even the commercials are stories. *Stories stir our emotions.* They impact us in ways that precepts and propositions never do.[120]

And what communicates more as a story than movies do? At the *78th Annual Academy Awards,* which aired on Sunday, March 5, 2006, on ABC, Sid Ganis, the president of the Academy of Motion Picture Arts and Sciences, said:

---

[119] Robinson, *Biblical Preaching,* 140.
[120] Warren, "Preaching for Life Change," 18, 19.

Stop Preaching and Start Communicating

> Tonight, as we look back at the absolute wonder of motion pictures, I think we realize that with all the magical technological advances that have brought movies to where they are today, everything we do on film is based on the most human of arts—the art of storytelling.
>
> In every culture, all around the world, storytelling is how people connect with one another. State-of-the-art technology will change, but state-of-the-heart storytelling will always be the same—even when the stories compel us to examine uncomfortable truths. Just look at our nominated films, both from the U.S. and around the world. They entertain us, of course, but they also give us a new understanding of the world, both past and present.
>
> Gregory Peck, a president of the academy and one of our greatest actors, said of his craft, "We are the salesmen of the story"…and modern-day storytellers have much to say. And by the way, I bet you none of the artists nominated tonight have ever finished a shot for a movie and stood back and said, "That's gonna look great on the DVD!" Because there is nothing like the experience of watching a movie in a darkened theater, looking at images on an eye-enveloping screen, with sound coming at you from all directions, sharing the experience with total strangers who have been brought together by the story they are seeing.[121]

I have never met anyone who doesn't enjoy listening to a good story. And I'm convinced that's why God decided to write more than three-quarters of the Bible in narrative form. I also think it's why Jesus' primary mode of communication was narrative.

> I think television has forced us to story. I think television has forced us to take a serious look at the parables of Jesus as a way of communicating. In the past, I think when we did didactic preaching and teaching, the full weight was on the preacher or

---

[121] *78th Academy Awards*, Sid Ganis, ABC, 5 March 2006.

teacher and almost no weight was on the person doing the listening. One of the things that story and image does is it forces the audience, the congregation, to invest in thought. They don't leave with the thing wrapped up for them and think *Look at how Jesus tells His stories. I mean, He tells a parable and walks away....* Our temptation is to say, "Now let me tell you why this happened and why this man did...." We'll explain it. Jesus doesn't, because the nature of a parable, the nature of a story, is you let the story carry its own weight, and we're not used to doing that. But that's the way it happens on television and in movies.[122]

Here are 3 ways to introduce story into your communication style:

Get rid of the points. As was discussed in Chapter 5, stop running down a shopping list of points by saying "Point 1 is...and point 2 is...and point 3 is...." Instead, embrace a more narrative style of communication by communicating conversationally with moves that seamlessly link to each other. By the end of the message, people can think about what they heard and be able to connect all of the moves together and see how those individual moves tell one story.

Introduce the message with a dramatic skit. This is effective, even in small churches. I've done it, complete with wardrobe and props, in churches with 75 people, and it has worked beautifully. A 5- to 10-minute skit before the message can not only complement but actually bring to life what you're going to share.

Communicate first-person narratives. A first-person narrative is simply taking a biblical character and telling that particular biblical story through his or her eyes. In the first one I did, I chose to be David and told the story of the incident that took place between him and Bathsheba (2 Samuel 11-12). Not only did I have a great time preparing for it and doing it, but the reaction from the crowd was extremely positive. It was refreshing for me to communicate a Bible message in a

---

[122] Robinson, "Preaching in a Television Age."

different way. And it was equally refreshing for the audience to see and hear a different approach being taken in communicating a biblical message.

I'm not recommending that you do first-person narratives every week. But I am suggesting that you sprinkle them throughout the year to add some variety for both you and your audience.

Torrey Robinson, who has written a book on how to do first-person narratives, has this to say:

> There's so much in the Bible that is narrative and even parts of the Bible that aren't narrative that can be told in a narrative fashion. First of all, it's worth doing it the way the Bible does it.... It's silly to take a story and make it into precepts, because the audience hears stories better. If you have a choice between a more didactic kind of approach or a story approach, people will hear the story better. I find when I do first-person sermons that frequently people with young kids will say, "Let me know when your next first-person is and we'll have our kids stay in the service." On the other hand, no matter how good my didactic or precept message is, as of yet I have never had a parent come up to me and ask if their kids could stay in the service. So the story approach or first-person narrative is definitely a more audience-friendly approach.[123]

I recommend reading three great books on the subject:

- *Effective First-Person Biblical Preaching: The Steps from Narrative to Sermon* by J. Kent Edwards
- *Telling Stories to Touch the Heart* by Reg Grant and John Reed
- *It's All In How You Tell It: Preaching First-Person Expository Messages* by Haddon Robinson and Torrey Robinson

---

[123] Personal interview with Torrey Robinson.

Picture Power

This isn't necessarily a term that's used in television, but it's what makes television so appealing. The mediums of radio and print simply don't have the advantages of television. Radio is audio without pictures, and print is pictures without audio. Television, on the other hand, engages sight, sound, motion and emotion. If one still picture is worth a thousand words, how much more are moving pictures worth?

To keep you engaged, television will show you a particular scene from a number of different angles. They will zoom in, zoom out, tilt up, tilt down, pan left, pan right and do everything they need to do to make what you're watching as engaging and appealing as possible. As communicators, we should, and can, do the same. If there's an image we're trying to get across, we have the ability to show that image from all the different angles that television can. We can zoom in and show all its detail. We can zoom out and show our audience the bigger picture. We can tilt up, tilt down, pan left, pan right—we can make it as visually appealing as we like by the words we use.

What makes television so appealing is that it is a sight and sound communications medium that engages all five of the viewers' senses. And our job is to communicate in the same manner, with lots of pictures, engaging the five senses. It's a sure recipe for making great communicators.

As discussed in Chapter 5, the idea is to take your moves and turn them into pictures. You don't want to leave your moves as abstractions. You want to make your moves concrete. You want to make them specific. You want to turn them into pictures. Haddon Robinson offers some very helpful examples:

> For instance, let's suppose you wanted to get a move across, and the point was all of us are sinners. You say that, and nobody sits there and says, "Yeah, that's right." But if you're going to take sinners, one of the things you're going to have to do as a preacher is to take theology and bring it down to life. So out of what you know, when you think of the word *sinner*, what are some of the images that are behind the word *sinner*?

How do we use that word? Well, there's the term "missing the mark" that has to do with a hunter or a bowman shooting at a target. Rebellion, okay that's another one, rebellion.... Trespassing, when you think of trespassing, what comes to your mind? Hunting, of course. You're after the deer. It's your deer. I mean, it's got your name on it. The deer jumps over the fence, and then you see a sign that says "No Trespassing." You have a choice to make. That's your deer, and there's a sign that says "No Trespassing." You decide to go after the deer and you step over the fence—that's trespassing. What you have behind each of those words is an image. What you need to do is take that image and expand it, so people can see it.

Another thing you want to do in a move is sometimes to think about how people experience what you're talking about. You step over the boundary, how do you experience that?... For example, you step over the boundary in a conversation, a friend is not there, and you make a cutting remark about them. You know you shouldn't do it, but you don't say anything else; you just let it go. Call it a slip of the tongue, I don't care what else you call it, the Bible calls that trespassing; that's sin. Or you're with a group of people, you, your wife, other people and their wives. You find yourself looking at the other man's wife. In your mind you're undressing her, and you know if he found out what you were doing he would beat your face in. If you thought he was doing that to your wife, you'd hit him.... Call it fantasy. I don't care what you call it, that's stepping over the boundary. You know you've done it. That's what the Bible means by sin. So, what you're doing in all these cases is you're working with image. You have to start with theology, but you have to move it to image.[124]

If you're interested in saying a lot with a few words, show—don't tell; communicate with pictures, so that people can see what you're saying.

---

[124] Robinson, "Preaching in a Television Age."

Pitch Ahead

A more familiar expression used for this term is *coming up next*. When you pitch ahead, you're telling someone what's coming up next. And everybody is very familiar with the term *coming up next*, which is constantly used in television. It is equivalent to what we would call a transition in the world of spoken communication. It is used a lot in documentary shows like *60 Minutes*, *20/20* and *Dateline*, basically saying, "We just discussed one angle of the story, but coming up next we're going to look at this from a different angle." In short, this technique is used as a mile marker to show the viewer what the program has covered up to that particular point and where it is going. And again, you have to remember that everything in television is done for one reason only: to keep you tuned in, so you won't pick up that remote and switch to another channel.

We should also take transitions very seriously when communicating. Because they happen so often—between the introduction and the first move, between the other major moves, before the application, and finally between the application and the conclusion—we have to be sure that our transitions are full and complete, not leaving any doubt in the listeners' minds as to where we've been and where we're going. There can be five or six transitions in an average message, which means if you're not careful in crafting your transitions, there are at least five or six places where you can lose people. So at those transition points you need to slow down; tell people that you're going to make a turn up ahead; show them you've flicked on your turn signal, you've now come to a complete stop, you're looking both ways by reminding them where you've been and where you're headed; and once you see that the way is clear and that everyone is tracking with you, you can proceed to make your turn and continue on your journey.

> It is easy to lose people in the curves. As you transition from introduction to the text to your point to your application, give people some sort of indication that you are making a transition…. Transitions give people a chance to catch back up with you. They provide the audience with an opportunity to rejoin

the discussion. They may have lost track of where you are for a variety of reasons, many of which you may have no control over. But by slowing down in the curves, by creating a break in the action, they are able to re-engage.[125]

PLAN AHEAD

If there's one thing that television is always doing (and I do mean always), it's planning ahead. They're always working on the details of what will be coming out in the next three to six months, based on a plan that they have in place for the whole year. Planning ahead helps you tremendously in preparing your cross promos, which we discussed earlier, and your teasers, which will be discussed shortly. In fact, you can only prepare teasers and cross promos if you have a plan in place. The key is to plan ahead. It'll do wonders in organizing mentally and visually where you're headed for the whole year.

But planning ahead doesn't just benefit you. It also benefits your teams. It benefits your worship team because they can now make the appropriate song selections around the individual messages that you're preparing. If your church does skits before the messages, it benefits your writers and performers. The plan that you take the time to prepare becomes your church's road map for the upcoming year, which helps everyone to work toward the same goals.

PLAYBACK

Playback in television—rewinding and playing back what you just saw—is what we call in the oral communication world *repetition*—saying the same thing in the same words. Television uses the playback feature often. In sports, for example, if a goal that was scored is being questioned, the officials will rewind that particular play and play it back to confirm that the puck actually did cross the goal line.

There is one area where you should use this playback idea: when you're communicating the one big idea of your message. As mentioned

---

[125] Stanley and Jones, *Communicating for a Change*, 157, 158.

in Chapter 7, the main point should be repeated no less than three times and preferably five or six times during the message. But here's the key: it must be done in exactly the same way, using exactly the same words, every time you say it. You do this for two reasons:

- It communicates to the people listening to you that this is the most important thing you're going to say throughout the message.
- It ensures that people remember it the way you said it.

The commercial taglines we looked at in Chapter 7, such as "Good to the last drop," "Don't leave home without it" and "Just do it," have stuck with us for years because they were repeated in exactly the same way, using exactly the same words, every time we heard them.

PROGRAM NAME

The reputation of a TV program is wrapped up in its name. If a program does well, its name is well received. If a program does poorly, the name goes down with it. Television producers follow three guidelines when choosing program names. They make sure the names are:

- short;
- memorable; and
- say something about the actual program.

Notice how the following program names fit that criteria: *American Idol, Dancing with the Stars, The Apprentice, Wheel of Fortune, Jeopardy, Entertainment Tonight, 20/20.*

When I travel, I like to check out the names of churches. Here are three in particular that caught my attention and made me chuckle:

- *Mountain of Fire and Miracles Ministry*
- *El Yehovah Deliverance Worship Centre*
- *Christ's Chosen Church of God International—Where Jesus is Real [Miracle Depot]*

I'd like to suggest that the criteria used in television when choosing a program name works for choosing a church name as well. Make sure it too is:

- short;
- memorable; and
- communicates something about the church.

In addition, keep in mind:

- Your name, when possible, should say something positive about your church.
- Try to avoid acronyms. In the business world, for every IBM there are hundreds of meaningless examples.
- Choose an upbeat and cheerful name instead of a bland one.
- Simple is better than complicated.
- Less is better than more.
- A logo and a symbol are better than just a logo. Again, businesses do this well: there is Prudential and the rock, McDonald's and the golden arches, Nike and the swoosh, CBS and the eye.

One final suggestion is to drop the denomination from the name. Whether your church is Baptist, Presbyterian or Pentecostal, there's no need to include that in the name, because it doesn't mean anything to seekers. Seekers go out looking for a church, not a denomination. Some of the biggest churches in America, such as Willow Creek Community Church, Saddleback Community Church, Northpoint Community Church and Fellowship Church, make no mention of the denomination they belong to in their church names.

STILL FRAME

In television, a still frame is used to focus the viewers' attention on a particular image. In essence, the video is paused on a certain shot to draw attention to it. We should get into the habit of doing the same when communicating orally. There's power in pausing, especially when you've driven home a certain point that you want to sink into the listeners' hearts. Simply pause and say nothing. When you mean what you say, you can pause on purpose! And there's more power in pausing than there is in meaningless sounds like *umm*, *uhh*, *so* and *er*. In some cases, communicators will throw in a few *Amen*s and *Praise God*s as fillers rather than pausing, because of discomfort with any silence.

They're afraid they may come across as unprepared. In fact, speakers who can properly pause during a message display the exact opposite to the audience. They communicate that they have enough self-control to use the power of the pause to add emphasis to their messages.

STORY TITLE

Television does a great job in coming up with story titles. As in choosing program names, they strive to make story titles short, memorable and say something about the story. Message titles are also very important. It's the first thing that people connect with before they hear the actual message, so the key is to tease them with a title that makes them want to hear the message. And again, message titles should be short, memorable and relate in some manner to the big idea. Following those three guidelines should allow you to come up with message titles that will encourage people to hear what you have to say. Here are some examples to get you thinking: "Small but Dangerous," from James 3:2-12; "Use It or Lose It," from Matthew 25:14-30; "Robbing God," from Malachi 3:8-12; and "Don't Just Do Something, Sit There," a message from Luke 10:38-42 that will be highlighted in Chapter 10. These message titles work because they start people asking questions like *What does that mean?* The title should not give substantial insight into what will be shared—or there would be no need for the message. Instead, it should tell them just enough to tease them into wanting to hear the message. Ed Young Jr. states:

> Titles should be tantalizing and build interest for your message before you speak one word. It's just like fishing: if you want to catch a big bass, you have got to have a lure that turns the bass's head. It's easy to come up with seminary-friendly titles like "Sanctification and Social Ethics" or "Unrealized Eschatology in a Postmodern World." You may love these titles, but they are not very audience friendly. To most people in your church, it sounds like you're from another planet. It is vitally important that everyone in your audience can connect with your title.[126]

---

[126] Young Jr., "Keys to Creative Communication," 14.

Teaser

In television, the teaser is used to do just that—tease you about something that's coming soon. Many teasers run during the latter part of the summer months to prepare you for the new shows that will start airing in the fall. As you may be aware, television launches all of its new programs every year in September, because that's when children, teens and young adults return to school and people get back into a regular routine. These teasers will start by saying something like "New, this fall on NBC! Don't miss…" or "Coming this fall on NBC.…" Networks will run these teasers during morning, mid-day and prime-time programming to make sure a wide audience sees them. They make them as captivating as possible, hoping your response will be "I gotta see that!"

Teasers called movie trailers are also shown in theaters before the feature film. If they hook you with a fast-paced, highly produced teaser, you'll make a mental note of the date that movie hits the theaters so that you'll be there to watch it.

If you're wise, you'll also begin to use teasers in your church, because they're a great tool to promote what will be happening soon. Let's say, for example, you have a new 4- or 6-part sermon series starting soon and you've already mapped out what each message will deal with. You have the big ideas and the titles of the individual messages, as well as the overall title of the series. You can tease your audience by mentioning it in the bulletin, running a teaser on the video screens before the service begins and making a quick mention of it while the announcements are being shared. Have a banner ad pop up on the home page of your Web site with the name of the series, what it's going to deal with and the date it's going to start. Another effective way is to produce a 60-second video teaser in the form of a commercial about the series and run that during your announcements. Obviously your church would have to be equipped with the proper equipment to produce these teasers, but with the technology we have today and with the wealth of talent we have sitting in our congregations, you'd be amazed at how simple something like this is to put together. And it will have a much greater impact than simply mentioning it during the announcements or in the bulletin. Remember, networks use teasers to get people talking about new shows that are coming soon, which is exactly the result you want.

Time

Television is all about time. In a television control room there are clocks everywhere. There are big clocks, little clocks, digital clocks, face clocks, even stopwatches, and there's a production assistant who does nothing but look at the clock and count down the time remaining in the current segment on the air. There's also a floor director, whose primary role is to continually signal the on-air talent how much time they have left to speak before cutting to the next element. And in television it's not about minutes; it's about seconds. Everything is timed to the second. A 30-second commercial runs for 30 seconds and no more. And the same goes for any other element that airs on television, because in television, time rules. And because producers know that every second counts, they make the most of every one of them.

You also need to respect the time that's given to you and make the most of it. Don't waste it, because your audience may not give you a second chance. And remember, less really is more!

Vocal Inflection

Can you imagine watching a bunch of people on television deliver their lines in a monotone with no vocal variety whatsoever? How long do you think you would watch? My guess is not long. The same is true when communicating orally. We need to have vocal variety. We need to change the pitch of our voices when communicating. That's what vocal inflection is all about. Why is this so important? Because the enemy of delivery is monotony! Listen to the voice-overs of commercials and notice how much vocal variety there is in just one 30-second commercial. Now, if that's the case for one ad that lasts just half a minute, how important is *your* vocal variety for 35 minutes? Maintaining a variety of vocal inflections during your messages, such as saying certain things louder or softer at times and adding some punch to a word or phrase that needs emphasis, will help people stay tuned in and keep them from slipping into a mid-morning nap. The key is that your vocal inflections need to be varied throughout your message.

> Unfortunately, some preachers know no other way to emphasize their points, and as a result, their sermons sound like shouting matches. They confuse volume with spiritual power, thinking that God speaks only in the whirlwind. Like monopitch, the monotony on unvarying volume wears on a listener. In past centuries, preachers had to shout in order to be heard. Today, with the effective public address systems, shouting is no longer necessary, or even desirable. Emphasis comes through variety. Dropping your voice to a mere whisper can put an idea into *italics* as effectively as a loud shout. Intensity can be as effective as volume. Unfortunately many ministers use only one degree of force, whereas employing a wide range of volume—ranging from loud to soft—could enhance their delivery.[127]

A whole book could be written about television's tricks, but the goal of this chapter is to simply make you familiar with the more frequently used ones so that you'll be able to watch out for them and, more importantly, use them within your own communication style and ministry settings.

---

[127] Robinson, *Biblical Preaching*, 216, 217.

CLOSE-UP SHOT

🎥 THERE ARE SEVERAL TRICKS OF THE TRADE THAT TELEVISION USES TO KEEP PEOPLE TUNED IN. BECOME FAMILIAR WITH THEM. WATCH FOR THEM. AND MOST IMPORTANTLY, USE THEM.

9

CALL NOW!

*"The Bible was not given to increase our knowledge,
but to change our lives."*

—D. L. Moody—

"It can be yours for just three easy payments of $29.95! Operators are standing by. Call now and receive this special free gift bonus offer when you make your purchase." Whether it's an infomercial trying to sell you the latest kitchen gadget or a news series on the health hazards of smoking, there is one area where television excels, and that is in prompting viewers to act on what they see and hear. Everything in television revolves around this one thing—the call to action. Television producers don't just want viewers to hear their message; they want them to believe it and act on it. Companies advertise to make you believe their products are great and to get you off the couch and into the stores to buy them. The whole process can be summed up in three steps:

> Step 1: See this image, experience this feeling, feel this need. Step 2: Buy and consume this product. Step 3: Accept, by faith, that using or consuming this product will help you become like the people in the images.... Consumers tend to act toward a product as if it had a soul or a personality of its own.[128]

---

[128] Willhite and Gibson, (eds.). *The Big Idea of Biblical Preaching*, 87.

I'm hoping that you're seeing a strong parallel to what we as communicators of God's Word are called to do. We're not to simply inform; we're to transform. We're to be agents of change. We're not to just transfer information so that people will have more Bible knowledge, but we're to show people how to apply what the Bible says to every area of their lives. We're to remind them of James' often-quoted words that we're not just to be hearers of the Word but also doers (James 1:22). What's your goal in communicating God's Word?

When Your Goal Is to Inform

One thing they taught us in our sales and advertising classes was to produce messages that always include a call to action. We were taught not only to inform people but, more importantly, to have people act on what they heard. Now, that's not exactly what I found when I first started attending church. What I found were two basic approaches, both focused on transferring information. The goal was to increase Bible knowledge—to inform.

One of the approaches I was exposed to was to **teach the Bible to people.**

> The idea here is to teach the content of the Bible so that interested parties can understand and navigate their way through the Scriptures. This is usually the goal of the preacher or teacher who methodically and systematically teaches verse by verse through books of the Bible. This is the perfect approach for the communicator whose goal is to simply explain what the Bible means. Wherever we left off last week, we will pick it up again next week. This approach requires no creativity. This approach need not include any application.[129]

Those who communicate in this manner are mainly concerned with making sure they cover all of the material. It's basically like a biblical history class that you would take in seminary.

---

[129] Stanley and Jones, *Communicating for a Change*, 93.

The other approach I was exposed to was to **teach people the Bible**.

This goal differs from the first in that the communicator takes the audience into account as he plans his approach. After all, the goal is to teach **people**. Communicators who have embraced this goal are constantly looking for effective ways to impart biblical truth into the mind and heart of the hearer. This goal was behind the "three points and an application" approach to preaching. The multipoint sermon or teaching outline is a great approach for the communicator whose goal is to teach people the Bible. Outlining makes it easier for the average listener to follow along.[130]

In this type of approach, the communicator will use lots of alliteration and illustrations to make sure the audience understands and remembers the material.

The primary goal of both approaches is to transfer information. The goal is to inform, to increase Bible knowledge. Rick Warren expressed some concerns with this approach:

> In the first place it [the Bible] says that knowledge puffs up but love builds up, and the Bible says that increased knowledge without application leads to pride. Some of the most cantankerous Christians that I know are veritable storehouses of Bible knowledge, but they have not applied it. They can give you facts and quotes and they can argue doctrine, but they're angry, they are very ugly people. The Bible says that knowledge without application increases judgment. To him that knows to do good and doesn't do it, it is sin. So really, to give people knowledge and not get the application is a very dangerous thing.[131]

I'm not saying that information isn't important. But the question is *How much information is enough?* Haddon Robinson answers that

---

[130] Ibid., 94.
[131] Duduit, "Purpose-Driven Preaching," 9.

for us: "The basic principle is to give as much biblical information as the people need to understand the passage and no more. Then move on to your application."[132] Haddon Robinson says:

> There is a greater danger that lies in spending too much time on explanation and not going far enough into application. After preaching, I've often come away feeling I should have shown them in a more specific way how to do this. It is difficult for our listeners to live by what they believe unless we answer the question *How?*[133]

A Trip to the Bookstore

One day, I got in my car and drove to a nearby bookstore to check out their self-help section. I was amazed at what I found. Not only was it one of the largest sections in the store—strategically positioned right near the front—but the books on the shelves covered everything from how to control your anger to practical steps to genuine happiness. Here are some of the titles I found:

- *Change Your Mind and Your Life Will Follow*
- *Dealing With People You Can't Stand*
- *Everyday Greatness*
- *How to Make People Like You*
- *How to Make Someone Love You Forever*
- *Life Without Limits: Conquer Your Fears, Achieve Your Dreams and Make Yourself Happy*
- *Stuff Happens (and Then You Fix It): 9 Reality Rules to Steer Your Life Back in the Right Direction*
- *The Life Plan: 700 Simple Ways to Change Your Life for the Better*
- *The Purpose of Your Life: Finding Your Place in the World Using Synchronicity, Intuition and Uncommon Sense*
- *The Ultimate Secrets of Total Self-Confidence*

---

[132] Scott Gibson, ed., *Making a Difference in Preaching: Haddon Robinson on Biblical Preaching* (Grand Rapids, MI: Baker Books, 1999), 87.
[133] Ibid., 90.

Another book, which swept through North America in a major way and exploded off bookstore shelves, is *The Secret* by Rhonda Byrne. The book and DVD sold millions of copies and were featured in newspapers, magazines, radio and on some of the biggest shows on television, including *Today* on NBC, *The Early Show* on CBS, *Larry King Live*, *The CBS Evening News* with Katie Couric and *Oprah Winfrey*. It's all about the law of attraction. The book says:

> Everything that's coming into your life you are attracting into your life. And it's attracted to you by virtue of the images you're holding in your mind. *It's what you're thinking.* Whatever is going on in your mind, you are attracting to you.[134]

The book goes on to say, "If you see it in your mind, you're going to hold it in your hand...and that principle can be summed up in three simple words. *Thoughts become things!*"[135] Rhonda Byrne states that the creative process behind *The Secret* is taken from the Bible (Matthew 21:22 and Mark 11:24). According to Byrne, the three steps behind the creative process of *The Secret* are:

- ask;
- believe; and
- receive.

Here's my point: after spending 30 minutes in the self-help section of that bookstore, it became very obvious that people have a big interest in how-to books. The driving question that people have today is *How?* Before becoming a Christian, I devoured every how-to book I could get my hands on. But after I became a Christian and started reading the Bible, I realized the Bible truly is the best how-to book ever written.

Consider also the number of daily TV talk shows on the air and the millions of people who watch them. Why do they watch? Because

---

[134] Rhonda Byrne, *The Secret* (Hillsboro, OR: Beyond Words Publishing, 2006), 4.
[135] Ibid., 9.

they're searching for how to deal with the life questions they're wrestling with.

When Your Goal Is to Transform

Having read over 500 books on preaching, Rick Warren concluded, "The vast majority did not understand that preaching is about transformation, not information."[136] Rick went on to explain that to understand the purpose of preaching you have to understand two things: first, what is the purpose of God for man? And second, what is the purpose of God for the Bible? Rick says that God's purpose for man is wrapped up in Romans 8:29, where it says that God's purpose from the very beginning of time has been to make us like Jesus, to conform us to the image of His Son. "Not to make us gods, but to make us godly.... So He wanted to make us like Himself."[137] Rick adds that God's purpose for the Bible is found in 2 Timothy 3:16,17. Although, he says:

> People misread that verse most of the time. The purpose of the Bible is not for doctrine, not for reproof, correction or instruction in righteousness. Those are all "for this" in the Greek. For this, for this, for this, in order that. The purpose is *in order that*. So doctrine in itself is not the purpose of the Bible. Reproof in itself is not the purpose; correction, training are not the purpose. The bottom line is to change lives. "That the man of God may be thoroughly furnished unto every good work." So every message must be preaching for life change.[138]

If our messages are going to have impact, they're going to have to be application driven rather than information laden. "Preaching for life change requires far less information and more application. Less explanation and more inspiration. Less first century and more twenty-first

---

[136] Duduit, "Purpose-Driven Preaching," 7.
[137] Ibid.
[138] Ibid.

century."[139] In fact, Keith Willhite says that we are to aim at the application in the introduction:

> Get to the point—or at least hint at it—right up front. A good sermon introduction is a like a travel brochure—full of colorful photos that say, "Picture yourself here."...From start to finish, the sermon can and should aim at the response desired from the listener.... In order to aim at application from start to finish, we must begin in the introduction to face the listener with the issue, to orient the listener with the subject, and to entice the listener with the answer from God's Word.[140]

Rick Warren shares this same thought:

> The biggest thing that I would say about application is that every pastor eventually gets to application. I'm just saying he needs to start with it, not end with it. A lot of guys need to start where they end their sermon.[141]

Eugene Peterson, speaking about his paraphrase of the Bible, *The Message*, succinctly adds:

> There is too much Bible study these days and not enough Bible living. We've got these evangelical churches becoming so scholastic, and it has really killed the Bible. The thought of all these people trying to preserve the truth in Scripture—which is important to do, I am grateful for their work—but I wish more that we would be concerned about the livability of Scripture.... That is one thing that *The Message* can convey, that livability. And that is what pastors are for. Pastors are not professors; we are not trying to explain things, defend things—we are in the ball game trying to get people base hits.[142]

---

[139] Stanley and Jones, *Communicating for a Change*, 96.
[140] Willhite, "A Sneak Peek at the Point," 18, 17, 22.
[141] Duduit, "Purpose-Driven Preaching," 9.
[142] Duduit, "Understanding the Word," 25, 26.

Haddon Robinson says that if our messages don't make a difference in Monday morning's world, then they're not worth sharing.

> The truth we preach on Sunday morning has to work in Monday morning's world, or else it's not worth the time it takes to tell it. If the truth doesn't get dressed up in overalls, doesn't put on a skirt, doesn't wear a business suit, doesn't work out in the marketplace, then what you're telling them really doesn't touch life at all. So suggest an action. What can they do tomorrow as a result of the truth they heard today? How could they put it to work? Good preaching will suggest not only one action but maybe several different actions that people could apply as a result of hearing that particular truth.[143]

So What? Now What?

When you communicate to transform, there are two questions you have to make sure you answer for your audience—*So what?* and *Now what?*[144] When you answer the *So what?* question, you're showing your audience what difference the truth you shared with them is supposed to make in their lives. Answering the *Now what?* question shows them how to go about making that change. Look at it this way: *So what?* focuses on **what** they need to change, while *Now what?* focuses on **how** to make that change. *So what?* feeds the *Now what?* When your audience clearly and fully understands the difference that the truth you communicated is to make in their lives, it will inspire them to act and make the necessary behavioral changes to see that truth become real for them. Rick Warren says:

> The result of sound preaching is a changed character. It's a difference in my lifestyle, the way I act. So it's not simply enough to interpret the text. It must be applied in a practical way. I've had pastors say to me, "I just interpret Scripture and then I

---

[143] Robinson, "How Can I Speak So An Audience Will Listen?"
[144] Stanley and Jones, *Communicating for a Change*, 97.

leave the application to the Holy Spirit." That's not good enough. Howard Hendricks says, "Interpretation without application is abortion." When you study the New Testament, you realize that it's almost all application. Look at the Sermon on the Mount, how much of that is practical? 100 percent.... The book of James, 100 percent application. But even the most doctrinal book, which is Romans, 16 chapters, half of it is application. There are eight chapters of doctrine, and there are eight chapters of application. Ephesians, half of it is doctrine, and half of it is application. Colossians is half doctrine and half application. Galatians is almost all application. Jesus did not say, "I have come that you may have information." And without application your sermon simply becomes a harmless discussion.[145]

Rick suggests three ways we can communicate God's Word more practically:

Always aim for a specific action. What specifically do you want them to do? Rick often suggests a practical homework assignment with something specific for his audience to do.

Tell them why. Explain to your audience what this change will do for them. It's necessary to explain the benefits of the change if you ultimately want your audience to make the change you're recommending.

Show them how. Here again, Rick reminds us that the best-selling books today are the how-to books, the self-help books. That being the case, Rick says that it's critical to show your audience how to apply the truths you share with them. He suggests giving them a step-by-step procedure to follow, because "Nothing becomes dynamic until you become specific."[146] Rick shared that he has sat through many sermons where he's written the letters YBH off to the side of his notepad. The letters stand for *Yes, but how?* He would hear someone say, "Men, you need to be bet-

---

[145] Warren, "How to Communicate to Change Lives—Part 1."
[146] Ibid.

ter husbands." And he would write YBH—*Yes, but how?* "You need to be better fathers." *Yes, but how?* "Ladies, you need to be better wives." *Yes, but how?* "You need to pray more." *Yes, but how?* Rick reminds us that "Exhortation without explanation leads to frustration" and that "we need less 'ought to' preaching and more 'how to' preaching."[147]

What makes the Bible so special is the fact that it is truly the best self-help book ever written. And when you consider that 72% of Christ's words were words of application,[148] a person who begins to read the Bible quickly realizes that he can use and apply the information in his life in practical ways.

A Book About God

Ultimately, the Bible is a book about God. Haddon Robinson reminds us that the Bible isn't a textbook about ethics or a manual on how to solve personal problems. When we study the Bible, we need to ask *What is the vision of God in this passage?*[149] We need to remember that God is in every passage; we simply need to look for Him. To do that, Haddon suggests four questions we need to ask:

- What is the vision of God in this particular text?
- Where precisely do I find that in the passage? (The vision of God is always in the specific words and the life situation of the writer or the readers.)
- What is the function of this vision of God? What implications for belief or behavior did the author draw from the image?
- What is the significance of that picture of God for me and for others?[150]

When we've identified that vision in a passage, Haddon says that it's important to look at the human factor as well. We need to consider how the people in the biblical text should have responded to this vision. We also need to look at how they **did** respond. And should this vision

---

[147] Ibid.
[148] Young Jr., "Keys to Creative Communication," 13.
[149] Robinson, *Biblical Preaching*, 94.
[150] Ibid.

have made any practical difference in their lives? Haddon says, "This human factor is the condition that men and women today have in common with the characters in the Bible."[151]

Therefore, when applying a passage, we need to see what the passage reveals about God and the way people responded and lived before Him. In turn, we need to look for those same factors in people's lives today.[152] To do that, Haddon suggests we ask these questions:

- Where do the dynamics of the biblical situation show up today?
- So what? What real difference does this truth about God make to me or to others? What difference should it make? Why doesn't it make a difference?
- Can I picture for my listeners in specific terms how this vision of God might be one they need in a particular situation? Would there ever be an occasion when someone might come to me with a problem or need and I would point them to this passage and this truth? Listeners feel that a sermon is relevant when they can say, "I can *see* how that would apply to my life."[153]

TESTIMONIAL POWER

It's clear that for a message to be effective, it needs to relate biblical truth to life. But how can you find out if people are applying what they hear and if it's actually making a difference in their lives? There's only one answer—allow them to give a testimony of how that particular truth has changed their lives.

If there's one thing I've learned in producing television commercials, it's this: testimonials sell products! In fact, testimonials have the power to sell anything. I'm sure you've seen the ads with people telling you how great their all-in-one power tool is or how amazed they are about their new mop. If you happen to catch a commercial or infomercial enough times, you're going to eventually order the product. Why? Because having seen the before and after shots and heard how thrilled

---

[151] Ibid., 94, 95.
[152] Ibid., 95.
[153] Ibid.

the person on screen is about the product, you will actually believe it can do the same for you. So you take down the 1-800 number, make the call and order it. In fact, there are *As Seen On TV* stores that carry only products that are advertised on TV.

Television also uses testimonials in a powerful way in many of the PSAs (public service announcements) that it produces. Whether it's a PSA for MADD (Mothers Against Drunk Driving), the Lung Association on the hazards of smoking, or an HIV awareness campaign, some of the most indelible PSAs ever produced were created using the power of the testimonial.

The people in your audience can experience that same impact when you introduce a testimonial as one of your moves during a message, either live or via video. There is incredible life-changing power when a person stands before a crowd and tells how a particular truth that he decided to apply to his life has made an enormous difference for him. The people listening will think *If it can work for him, it can work for me.* But here's the real beauty of the testimony—it doesn't come from you! Because you're seen as the person with all the answers, the fact that it doesn't come from you makes it that much more believable. In other words, you don't have to bear the burden of trying to poke and push and jab your audience to do anything. They hear you do that enough. You can actually take a back seat and let the testimonial sell the truth on its own.

APPLICATIONS THAT TRANSFORM

Let's look at a couple of samples from two great communicators, Joseph Stowell and Andy Stanley. What I want you to look for in both applications is how they engaged the audience, primarily with the use of story, in such a way that the transformation process was already taking place while the people were listening to the message. Also note how they both use humor as was discussed in Chapter 4 in a subtle, yet very effective manner, while never taking their eye off the point they want to get across. The main texts that Stowell and Stanley used are parallel passages that have to do with trusting God.

In a message entitled "Followership" taken from Matthew 4:18-22, Joseph Stowell identifies a mark of following Jesus as being a "netless" believer, and he challenges his people by asking them a key question that he repeats throughout this particular move:

> Followers of Christ are netless believers. As I was thinking about this text, I thought *As long as Peter and Andrew hung on to their nets they were going nowhere with Christ.* Look at your hands. What are the nets in your hands? Look at them. What are those things that are presently in your grip that intimidate and prohibit your non-negotiated willingness to be a follower of Christ? Before they could follow Christ, for them, they had to drop their nets and follow Him. What is a net? Listen carefully: a net is anything in my life that inhibits or prohibits my non-negotiated commitment to following Him.
>
> I could give you my shortlist of nets that I struggle with. I wonder what your shortlist is like? Maybe for some of us it's things. Having been absorbed into a culture that celebrates the worth and value of things that moths and rust destroy and that thieves break in and steal, as Christ said, we tend to think that to accumulate things stacks up our sense of significance. And we think *You know, if I really become a follower of Christ maybe I'll have to give up some things. Maybe I'll have to share them. Maybe I'll have to give them away to someone in greater need than I am. I don't know if I want to yield things.* And it becomes a net, and you keep it in your grip and you can't follow.
>
> Maybe it's people. Maybe your net is someone you like a whole lot. And just hanging around with them brings you a great sense of significance and security. Yet, you know good and well that if you become a true follower of Christ it will lead you to values and to principles in your life that will set a distance between you and this person. You don't want to forsake them and you don't want to kick them out of your life; you just know that to be a follower of Christ is going to set a little distance.
>
> Maybe it's somebody you don't like. Maybe it's that person that you like to hate. Maybe it's that person you like to feel bitter against. That person has used you, abused you, violated you; that person has hurt and offended you. And you know good and

well that to be a follower of Christ you're going to have to drop that net of hatred and bitterness and resentment and revenge and begin to process the path of forgiveness. Maybe that's your net.

Maybe it's the net of your plans. When I grew up, my parents will tell you that I thought I was going to be a doctor. In high school, in a meeting, I gave my whole life to Christ. I said, "Lord, You can have the whole of my life for whatever You want me to do." Of course I knew He wanted me to be a doctor, so it was kind of an easy thing to do. But obviously He had different plans for my life. And I'm here tonight to tell you that He had a better plan. A little bit later in life I became aware of the fact that anytime I'm around physical trauma, especially if there's blood involved, I have a problem.

We came home one night when the kids were little and the babysitter said, "Oh, your son fell down and cut his eye and I put a Band Aid on it." I took the babysitter home, came back, went up to the bedroom and I pulled the bandage back, and there was this gaping wound over his eye and I knew we had to take him to the hospital to get him sewed up. So up to the children's hospital in our town we went. Walked into the emergency room. Went into this little room. The doctor walks in and he says to my wife, "Sit down there at the end of the table." "And sir, if you'll come here, please, and put both your hands on your son's shoulders so he doesn't wiggle." I said, "Of course"; what are men for except to do this kind of thing? [*Laughter*] So I'm standing there and he takes the syringe, fills it up with anesthetic, pops the air out of it and proceeds 18 inches from my face to make two inserts directly into the wound of my son's eye with this anesthetic. There was a little physical response to that, but I tried to control myself, you know, really be a man. [*Laughter*] And then he pinched the wound to begin to stitch it, and I felt like *I cannot do this*, and the nurse looks at me and she says, "Sir, are you all right?" I said, "I'm fine." [*Laughter*] *Dear Lord, please forgive me, seriously Lord.* Well, she didn't believe me either, so she took me by the elbow out into the hall, in this children's hospital, puts me in a wheelchair in the hall, puts my head between my knees, and when I finally recovered some stability and sat up she said, "Can I get you to a hospital?" [*Laughter*] I'm here to tell you that Christ had a better plan for my life. I don't get sick when I preach! You do, but I don't. [*Laughter*]

Did you ever think He had a better plan? So what are those nets? Look at your hands. Look at them. For some of us maybe it's the net of fear. Fear of the unknown—*Where will He take me?* Did you ever come home and tell your kids you're going to take them out for a surprise that night? They begin to quake and ask, "Oh please tell us, just tell us exactly what you're going to do with us." Of course not. They skip on out. "Yay!" Why are they so excited? Because they know who's taking them out, that's why. They have no idea where they're going; they just know who's taking them there.

So what are your nets? And why would any of them be of greater value to you than Christ? You see, it's a matter of values. Really, think about that. And it's a matter of outcomes. What do you want your life to be like when it's over, when you step on the threshold and look in the rearview mirror? For Peter, Andrew, James and John, just imagine if they had clung to their nets and stuck to their boats. They would have looked back over their lives and there would be piles of slippery, slimy, scaly and sometimes smelly fish. That would have been their life. But instead, they dropped their nets, they left their boats, they followed Christ and they look in the rearview mirror and it's a world that's been impacted for eternity.

It's a matter of outcomes. What do you want when it's all over? Stacks of stuff? Or an enriched eternity? Because you are a follower of Christ. It's a matter of values. It's a matter of outcomes. What are those nets? Followers of Christ are netless believers.[154]

---

[154] Joseph Stowell, "Followership," *Looking to Jesus*, Preaching Today, cassette no. 178.

In a message entitled "Trusting Christ at All Cost," taken from Luke 5:1-11, Andy Stanley was telling a group of adults in a Sunday morning service how he applied the principle of the trustworthiness of God to a group of young teenagers at a summer camp retreat.

> This summer I wanted to explain this principle of trusting God to some teenagers. This is a hard thing to get across to a young person because they're so focused, like we all are, on what they have. And when they read the Bible it just looks like God is trying to mess up all their fun. And to be honest, I remember one time when I was 18, I had a friend and this friend was good-looking and he had a lot of money and he had a career and a car and he was going to be rich the rest of his life because of the way his family deal was worked out. I mean, he had it together and he was pretty immoral. You know, he had all these girls, and I could remember as an 18-year-old thinking *You know, Lord, I know I shouldn't say this, but I'd hate to witness to this guy and mess up his life.* [Laughter] *I mean, I know I should share Christ with him, but You know, from my little 18-year-old perspective, man, this guy's got it made.* I mean, that's how I thought, because when we're young, and even when we're older, we get so focused on what God has asked us to give up. And it's like, "I don't mind giving up my life for You, but shewww, he's got a lot to give up, and I'm not sure if I were him if I'd give it up, to be honest."
>
> So I'm sitting in my hotel room thinking *How do I explain this to teenagers?* So I was praying and I remembered when Peter Lord and Jack Taylor were here, Peter Lord did this little interchange thing on the stage, if you were here, with a lady. And so I began thinking about that and I came up with another version of the Peter Lord thing. So what I did, I went to the guy selling T-shirts and I borrowed $325 in 10s and 20s and 5s and I stuck all this small cash in my pockets, just packed my pockets full of cash. And so I was teaching this lesson and the kids were sort of paying attention you know, because it's like, "Here we go again, give up everything for God—I've heard this before."

And I said, "Okay, I want somebody here, a guy preferably, who has all the money they brought to camp with them to come up here." So this guy in the middle of the crowd of several hundred kids raises his hand and he comes up and he's got his wallet. And I said, "Now before you come up on the stage, two things: number one, do you trust me?" And I'd been there all week with them at camp and he said, "Yeah, I trust you, I trust you." And I said, "Number two, when you leave this stage you'll be better off than when you came on this stage." You'll remember that Peter Lord did that. I said, "When you leave this stage you'll be better off than when you came on this stage." All right, so he came up on the stage and I said, "Take all your money out." He takes it out and counts it—$226. Now, this is the end of camp, and I'm thinking *How much did he bring?* [*Laughter*] So he's got $226. He's got this cash and I said, "Put your wallet away and hold out the cash." He's standing there holding out the cash. And I said, "Here's the deal; I want you to give me all your money. I'm not going to give any of it back to you, but I'll give you what's in my pockets." And it got real quiet in the room. And he's looking out there; it's kind of like one of those game shows. He's looking out there—*What should I do?* You know, he's holding this money. And everybody starts yelling and cheering and all this stuff and I said, "Wait a minute, wait a minute, do you trust me?" "Yeah." "Yeah?" I said. "Okay, then just give me your money, and I'll give you what's in my pockets and I promise you, you'll be better off than when you came up here."

And here's the thing, when I started this interchange it's like God said, "Andy, do you remember when you only had to offer me $10, how easy it was? And then it was $20. Now that you're an adult, it's harder, isn't it?" And I said, "Lord, this is for the kids, okay. This doesn't have anything to do with me." [*Laughter*] It's like all of a sudden, I got this picture of me, not this kid, this picture of me that you know, when the stakes were low, it's like "Oh God, wherever You lead I'll go. I trust You with my whole life…na, na, na, na, na, na." But as I got older, and as I had more stuff, and as the risk factor seemed to rise and rise and rise, it's like now, "[Whoa] God, [Whoa, whoa, whoa, whoa, whoa]." And God said, "Wait a minute. Wait a minute. The issue is not what's in your hand. The issue is am I trustworthy? And if I'm trustworthy with $10, then I'm trustworthy with $10,000. The issue isn't the value of what's in your hand. The issue isn't the importance of what's in your hand, Andy. The issue is am I trustworthy? If I'm trustworthy, then it doesn't matter what I ask for, does it?" "No." So I'm trying to learn a lesson and trying to lead the group, you know.

So this goes on and on and on and on. So I said, "Okay, if you only had $10, would you do it?" "Yeah." I said, "Wait a minute. If you only had $10, what's the difference? Either I'm trustworthy or I'm not." So the kids were finally getting the point. This goes on and on and on and on and on. I'm teaching, and we're going back and forth, and all these kids are finally going, "Give him the money. Give him the money." And I'm going, "It's easy for them to say, isn't it?" [*Laughter*] It's like when we read a Bible story, right, "Don't do it, David! Don't do it!" See, it's easy for us. So, he finally put his money in his wallet and he sat down and he didn't give me his money. The girl in the front row says, "What's in your pockets?" So very slowly and methodically I start pulling out 10s and 20s and 5s and 10s and 20s and 5s and counting it. Well, once I passed $226 the kid's expression changed. And when I hit $300 it really changed. And when he realized he lost $99 by not trusting me, he was just overcome with grief.

Now, I'll never forget that as long as I live. I don't know if those kids will remember it, or even got it, but I got it. Because there I stood with God, arguing, but God's going, "But you don't know what's in My pockets. Trust Me!" "But God, this is the best relationship I've ever had." "But I know more about relationships than you do. Trust Me!" "God, my whole financial future...." "No, no, no, no, no, your whole financial future.... Trust Me! Trust Me! Trust Me!" And then you know what I did? I said, "I need another volunteer." What do you think they did? [*Laughter*] I mean, they're pulling out their money and yelling, "Oh, take me! Take me!" You know, they're rushing the stage. And I said, "[Whoa, whoa, whoa]." I said, "Why is it that so many of you want to volunteer?" You know why they wanted to volunteer? Because they had seen me in action, right? We've seen Him in action. What are we arguing about? Hey, in your life you've seen Him in action. What are you arguing about? I mean, just go outside and realize that we're living on a ball of dirt hanging in the middle of nowhere rotating around the sun. And it goes around every day and nobody gets up and worries, "Gee, I hope the sun comes up...shewww, there it is." Hey, we've seen Him in action, haven't we? Yet, we just continue to argue, because we're so focused on our little thing and we're not really focused on the faithfulness of our God.

Let me say this again, the value of what's in your hand is not even the issue. The issue is can you trust Him? And when He asks for that thing, for those plans, for that dream, for that education, for that marriage, for that future, for that relationship, can you trust Him? And the answer is absolutely yes! You can. And you see, what's at stake is not what's in your hand. What's at stake is what's in His pockets. That is, it seems risky to say yes, but it's far more risky to say no. Because you have a loving heavenly Father who has your best interest in mind, and to follow Him will cost you. But listen, not to follow Him will cost you far, far more.[155]

We need more doers in our churches and less hearers. This is why our messages need to have more application and far less information. John Maxwell makes a great observation:

---

[155] Andy Stanley, "Trusting Christ at All Cost," 1993.

Preaching to me is not an end in itself. I believe that for the great communicators, their whole perspective of communicating is to change lives and to move people from one point to the other with the assistance of God. People that are speakers, their goal is to look good. There is a world of difference between those two. A speaker, when he or she is done, their whole issue is *How did I sound, did people like me?* Whereas, a communicator, their whole perspective is *Did it change a life?* Communicators are other focused, while speakers are inward focused.[156]

Make it your goal to communicate to transform rather than to simply inform.

---

[156] Michael Duduit, "Leading Through Preaching: An Interview with John Maxwell," *Preaching* 13, no. 4 (January-February 1998): 17.

Close-Up Shot

- Communicate to transform rather than to simply inform.

10

UNTIL NEXT TIME

"Life is not measured by the number of breaths we take, but by the moments that take our breath away."

—Anonymous—

How often do you leave people breathless after your message concludes? I think that most of the time we leave them looking for the exit.

Television producers put a great deal of effort into how they conclude whatever they produce. They could decide to conclude abruptly, which in television they refer to as a cold ending, or they may choose to end with a soft fade or a piece of dramatic music. However they decide to conclude, they want to make sure that those final words and images have maximum impact.

Unfortunately, most messages on Sunday morning don't conclude with maximum impact but with minimum effect, simply because not enough conscious effort is put into them. In fact, every single communicator I interviewed for this book confessed that the one thing he was most unhappy with was his conclusions.

So, in this chapter I will suggest ways in which you can conclude your messages, give you some dos and don'ts and highlight two sample conclusions that were really well done.

Ways to Conclude

There are a number of ways to conclude a message. You can use the same method to conclude a message that you used to introduce it.

Quotation. If you started your talk with a quotation, you may want to bookend your message by closing with that same quotation.

Question. Challenge your audience with a question, or a even a series of questions.

Song. Choose an appropriate song that effectively magnifies all that was said during the message.

Story. Conclude with an engaging story that properly highlights the main idea of the message.

Text. If your passage is short, succinct and drives home the big idea of your message, you may want to conclude with your text.

Video Clip. A strong visual that effectively helps solidify the main idea of your talk is a great way to have that central truth linger longer in your audience's minds.

Visualization. This is a method that projects an audience into the future and pictures a situation in which they might apply the truth they just heard. This exercise allows listeners to imagine themselves in that situation, or one similar to it, before it ever takes place.[157]

Whichever way you choose to conclude your message, **your conclusion should do nothing else but drive home the big idea of your message.** As Haddon Robinson says, "Your conclusion should bring your main idea to a burning focus." In short, you want to leave the words of your main idea ringing in people's minds as they exit the church.

---

[157] Robinson, *Biblical Preaching*, 179, 180.

DOS AND DON'TS

Keep it short. The shorter a conclusion, the more effective it is and the more impact it will have. Try to target no more than two to three minutes for the conclusion, and anything shorter is better. Think for a moment how Mel Gibson ended his movie *The Passion of the Christ*. The final images included Mary holding Jesus, which resembled the famous Pietà sculpture by Michelangelo. It then faded to black, and I along with everyone else thought the movie was over. But then, 8 seconds later, we saw and heard the stone in front of the tomb roll away. The camera then panned across the tomb, showing the empty linens and ending on a close-up shot of a resurrected and living Christ. All of that took one minute and 20 seconds. And what gave that closing sequence even more impact was that not a single word was spoken. The ending was breathtaking! Don't let your conclusions drag on. Keep them short. If you go beyond the 3-minute mark, you've gone too long and have started preaching again.

Keep it simple. The last thing you want to do with your conclusion is complicate it and make it difficult to understand. You don't want to leave people confused, scratching their heads and trying to figure out what you just said. Instead, you want to be as clear and simple as you can be, so that everyone understands those important final words.

Drive home the big idea. Spend the final few moments driving home the central idea of your message and nothing else. Your conclusion is the one last chance you have to make the main idea of your message stick, so don't waste it! Your main idea is basically the answer to the question you posed in your introduction, and driving home your main idea in the conclusion is like saying to your audience, "Satisfaction guaranteed!"

Don't conclude with the application. Think back to when you were in school and at the end of the class the teacher would say, "Okay, for tomorrow I want you to read pages 32 to 50 in your text and do exercises 1 through 5." All you would hear throughout the class would be sighs of frustration. Also, to reinforce what was said in Chapter 9, you should be applying the truth you're sharing throughout the message, rather than just giving it some closing comments at the end. Remember, your conclusion should not apply; it should conclude.

Don't conclude with a poem. This method has been mocked enough among preachers, but it's still being done.

Don't conclude with a hymn. This is similar to the poem idea. Many people in your audiences today are not familiar with the hymns that you may consider to be anthems of the Church, so don't read or sing a hymn written in 16th-century English to conclude your message. Most people will not be able to relate at all to what you're reading.

Don't conclude with a prayer. Stop using a prayer to conclude your messages that lasts a number of minutes and literally prays the message back to the audience again.

Don't conclude with new material. The conclusion is not the place to add those tidbits of information that you wanted to add to the body of the message but couldn't find a place for.

Don't summarize. If you have to summarize what you said in your conclusion, then you didn't do a very good job in communicating your message. People end up tuning you out because they're thinking *You said that already.*

Don't tell your audience you're going to conclude. Don't say things like, "In conclusion…" or "Finally…." Can you imagine a commercial, news story, or movie ending by saying, "In conclusion…"?

Don't conclude without a conclusion. I've heard many messages where the pastor stopped talking and went into prayer without concluding in any way. I once was in a service where the pastor stopped talking, looked up at the congregation and said, "All right, as I mentioned at the beginning of the sermon, I'm feeling really tired today from spending all day yesterday renovating my basement, so we're going to stop here today." And when I asked one very well-known preacher, who will remain nameless, about effective ways to conclude a message, he answered, "I have found that sometimes people absolutely love it if, when it is time to stop, I look at my watch and I say, 'Oh, my time is gone.' And I simply stop." Do yourself a big favor and conclude with a conclusion.

CONCLUSIONS THAT TAKE YOUR BREATH AWAY

Here are examples of conclusions that leave you breathless. And both of them conclude with powerful stories that drive home the main idea of the message. The first conclusion is from Haddon Robinson and the second is from Andy Stanley.

Haddon Robinson's conclusion is taken from a message entitled "Don't Just Do Something, Sit There," based on the story of Mary and Martha found in Luke 10:38-42.

Martha, being a type A, obsessive-compulsive, frantically hurries about, trying to prepare a meal for Jesus and His disciples, while Mary chooses to sit at Jesus' feet and hear His Word. Throughout the message, Haddon emphasizes the big idea, which he says is the importance of simplifying our lives by reducing the busyness that prevents us from spending time with Jesus. His conclusion not only magnifies his big idea but masterfully brings it, as he often says, to a "burning focus."

> He didn't bring you to Himself to make you a slave. He brought you to Himself to make you a friend. The Sovereign Majesty of the universe enjoys fellowshipping with us. Mary chose the good part because that's what Jesus wanted when He came to their home that evening.
>
> Years ago, when I was in seminary, Dr. Harry Hagar, who was then a pastor of a Christian Reformed church in Chicago, came to the campus. One evening he told us a story of a couple in his church. It was a mother and her son. The father had died when the boy was young, and they had a very unique relationship. This was back before television, when folks would spend evenings listening to the radio or reading. And they often read to one another. They enjoyed good music and listened to it. They had a special relationship. When he was in his early twenties, he met a young woman at the church, fell in love with her, and they decided they wanted to get married.

Back then, in World War II, housing in our large cities was very difficult to get. And so the mother, knowing that they wanted to be married, said, "Look, we have a two-storey house, I can make an apartment in the second storey, and you and your bride can come and live in the first storey. It will give you a home, and you can be married." She said, "The only thing I ask is that we get a chance to spend some time together, because I'm going to miss the reading and the music." The boy said, "Mother, you can be sure of that; it's too important to me."

So they were married and for a while it continued on. He would stop by a couple of times a week and spend some time, and then, you know, he got busy. And there were days and actually weeks that would go by where there was no call from downstairs, just a brief glimpse. The relationship was not what it had been. And then his mother had a birthday. And the young man went out and bought his mother a lovely dress. He knew her size and he brought it to her on her birthday and handed her the package and said, "Mother, happy birthday!"

She opened it and looked at the dress. And she said, "Oh, son, thank you. I appreciate so much what you have done."

He said, "Mother, you don't like it."

She said, "Oh, yes I do. I do. It's my color. Thank you."

He said, "Mother, I got the sales slip and they told me I can take it back."

She said, "No, I do, I do. It is a lovely dress."

He said, "Mother, don't fool me. We've been together too long. What's wrong?"

The woman turned and she went to her closet and she said, "Son, I have enough dresses there to last me for the rest of my life. I guess all I want to say is that I don't want yours; I want you."

And somehow out of this quaint story of the long ago I hear God saying that to me. Of all of my busyness, "You better simplify life. Because ultimately, I don't want yours as much as I want you."[158]

The following is Andy Stanley's conclusion to the message entitled "When Things Seem Uncertain." The introduction of this message was featured in Chapter 4, and he doesn't answer the question that he asked in the introduction—*What do you do during those times in your life when things seem uncertain?*—until he gets to the conclusion. It's a great way to maintain tension and keep people on the edge of their seats.

Do you know what you do in the midst of uncertainty? It's simple. You live as a man or woman who is confident that God is with you. That's all you do. Pharaoh says, "I want to put you in charge of the whole deal." You just do what you would do if God was with you. The question, the grid, the lens, which we interpret all of life is this: in light of where I am right now, what would somebody in my circumstances do today if they were absolutely confident that God was with them? And then you just do that. What do you do when your job is uncertain? I'll tell what you do when your job is up in the air: you do whatever a man or woman would do whose job is up in the air who's absolutely confident that God is with you. What do you do when your marriage is breaking apart, you don't know where she is, you don't know where he is, you don't know if they're coming back, you're not even sure if you want them to come back, you're so mixed up emotionally, what do you do? It's very simple. You get up tomorrow morning and you ask yourself this question: *If I was absolutely confident that God was with me, what would I do?* And then you just do that! Because you don't have to know the future and you don't have to know the end of the story, because we can live every single day of our lives with this confidence—God is with me!

Jesus said it this way: "'I will never' what?

---

[158] Haddon Robinson, "Don't Just Do Something, Sit There," *The Empowered Communicator*, Preaching Today, cassette no. 138.

(Audience) "Leave you or forsake you."
Let's say that again. "I will never…. "
(Audience) "Leave you or forsake you."

You know what that means? Tonight, as you sit here, and tomorrow, you have no idea what's going on. Tonight, you're going to go home thinking one thing is going to happen, and something else is going to happen. In that moment you do not need to know how it's going to work out. You do not need to know the end of the story. All you need to know is this: God is with me. You say, "Andy, Andy, Andy, that's no answer." It's the only answer, because God is in control and He's working out His will, His way, and we have been called to follow, and sometimes the only way to follow is to just do the next right thing in light of the fact that God is with you.

Sandra and I have three children; they're nine, eight and six, two little boys and a little girl. And when we had our first son, Sandra got real sick, and it was Andrew—we didn't know who it was yet. Andrew was distressed and so they had to do an emergency C-section; scared me to death. You know, first time going through all this and they whisk her away and I couldn't go in there with her, and I never cried so hard in my life as an adult, when they took her away. I didn't know what was going to happen, and they weren't sure, and they weren't telling me anything. You know how it is in the hospital, let's just keep the important people ignorant. So I'm just cryin'. I had a good friend with me, and we're just huggin' and I'm cryin'. They just took her away, I didn't know what was going to happen to her or the child; so anyway, we got through that.

Then we get pregnant again, so this time it's going to be normal we hope, and so she has to have another C-section because she had this first C-section. And we had to go to these childbirthing classes…ugh. That was just wonderful. That made me really want to go through this. [*Laughter*] But the doctor said, "It's not going to be like that. This is like surgery, so you're going to come in and watch me do surgery on your wife. We're going to cut her open and pull the baby out. It's going to just be wonderful, so you can come in there and watch that." [*Laughter*] And I said, "Do I have to?" And she's like, "Uh huh, yeah." So I'm sitting on a stool, and there's my wife on this bed and there's this curtain, you've been there. And so here's the curtain, and on this side is her head, and on this side is the rest of her. And over here is the anesthesiologist and he's got tanks, and so I'm sitting right here and I can see both worlds of this curtain, you've been there? And I'm watching them and saying to my wife, "Can you feel that?...You can't feel that?" [*Laughter*] I'm just dying. You've been there. And I'm doing my breathing exercises because I'm about to pass out, [*Laughter*] because they cut her open and they put this tape, and then they...this is gross, and if you have not had children, you may put it off after this...but they start bringing part of her insides out and they lay it over on her belly to get to the baby. [*Laughter*] And the doctor starts telling me what it is, and I'm like *I don't want to know! Just put it there*, you know. [*Laughter*] I couldn't get over the fact that she couldn't feel this, because she's fine and she's talking to me, asking how it's going, and I'm going, "Ooooh, it's going great. Don't lift that curtain! Don't look!" [*Laughter*]

So anyway, we're going through this whole deal and I am so stressed out and I'm praying, "O Lord..." Keep praying, you know. Meanwhile, over here in surgery land our doctor, Dr. Lion, who delivered all of our children, he and the nurses are over here just chitchattin'. They talked about their pets. He and the other doctor talked about a fishing trip. I'm over here breathing hard, praying, holding her hand, wanting to turn it up to 11, you know. [*Laughter*] And honestly I just wanted to go, "Hey, hey, hey, focus! Focus! This is my wife. Focus on what you're doing!" [*Laughter*] They're just "Taa, ta ta ta taa ta ta ta daa, my oh my...." You know why? Because it's no big deal to them, and I'm breathing hard about it and I had to get up and walk around—you know, you've been there. Well, do you know what I realized? You see, that's Dr. Lion's world. That's what he does. He does it three times a day sometimes. For me it's brand new and I'm dying. For him he could almost do it in his sleep because he's done it so many times. Listen, in this environment, he's the master. In this environment, I'm the stranger.

Let me tell you something about your God. When it comes to uncertainty, He's the Master. He's done this so many times. You're the stranger, it's new, oh my God what's going to happen? He's going, "Oh man, I can do this in my sleep. Listen. I love uncertainty! I created the world out of uncertainty. I brought out of fruition the nation of Israel out of uncertainty. I sent a Messiah into uncertainty. I forgave you of your sins in the midst of uncertainty. I raised Him from the dead in the midst of uncertainty. This is not a big deal to Me." Take a deep breath and live as a man or a woman who's confident that God is with you.[159]

What made these two conclusions so effective is that they used those concluding moments to drive home the main idea of their message. The result? It left their audiences breathless.

---

[159] Stanley, "When Things Seem Uncertain."

CLOSE-UP SHOT

🎥 YOUR CONCLUSION SHOULD ACCOMPLISH ONE THING AND ONE THING ONLY: IT SHOULD DRIVE HOME THE MAIN IDEA OF YOUR MESSAGE.

Conclusion

In the movie *Sister Act*, Whoopi Goldberg plays Delores Van Cartier, a Reno, Nevada, lounge singer who is unknowingly dating a mobster. When she goes to him to break off their relationship, she inadvertently becomes a witness to a murder and narrowly escapes from his thugs. A police lieutenant, Eddie Souther, is charged with keeping her safe until she can testify in court about her former boyfriend's activities. She reluctantly goes into hiding as a nun in a Catholic convent, called St. Katherine's Convent, where she wears a habit and is given the name Sister Mary Clarence.

She detests the austere lifestyle of the convent and grates on the nerves of the Mother Superior, who, to keep her out of trouble, puts her in the convent's choir, which is lifeless and has a tone-deaf leader. But this is where Whoopi shines. She takes over the choir and puts a new touch on old hymns. At the service where Whoopi is introduced as the new choir director, she leads the choir in a swinging up-tempo version of "Hail Holy Queen." People outside the church hear the new contemporary sound and decide to walk in during the service. Even the altar boys begin to tap their toes. But one person isn't impressed with the new sound—Mother Superior. In fact, immediately after the service, Mother Superior calls Whoopi into her office and lets her have it, while the sisters from the choir are all gathered outside Mother Superior's office door, listening in.

Mother Superior: "Girl groups? Boogie-woogie on the piano…what were you thinking?"

Whoopi: "I was thinking more like Vegas, you know, get some butts in the seats."

Mother Superior: "And what next? Popcorn? Curtain calls? This is not a theater or a casino!"

Whoopi: "Yeah, but that's the problem, see. People like going to theaters and people like going to casinos. But they don't like coming to church. Why? Because it's a drag! But we can change all that; see, we could pack this joint."

Mother Superior: "Through blasphemy? You have corrupted the entire choir!"

Whoopi: "How can you say that? I've worked my butt off with these women. They've given up their free time to do this and they're good. I mean, Sister, we can rock this place!"

Mother Superior: "Out of the question. As of tomorrow, Mary Lazarus resumes her leadership of the choir."

I've watched that movie several times. It's actually one of my favorites, simply because I can totally relate to how Whoopi felt, and perhaps you can, too. In fact, it's the reason I wrote this book about communication principles you can learn from television, to help you communicate God's Word more effectively. If you really think that you can continue to communicate God's Word the way it was done 50, 30, or even 20 years ago, then you're not in touch with what's going on around you. You need to stop preaching and start communicating.

Haddon Robinson summed it up beautifully:

> We always live in the light of His fire. He doesn't need us. He doesn't need folks who are sure they are going to do it the way they have always done it. He passes by churches. He blows out lamps. He moves on to other things. The only question is whether we're going to move with Him or stay where we are

and let the fire fall someplace else. That is the challenge. And if we do not rise to it, someone else will. God's work will be done with us or without us. I would pray that as men and women of faith we shall be where God is, to do what God wants, to penetrate our society on every level, so that when our generation has served its time, we shall have made the impact for Jesus Christ that He has called us to make.[160]

If you closely study how Jesus communicated to His audiences, you'll see He did it in all the ways mentioned throughout this book. His introductions were engaging. He spoke in everyday words that everyday folks understood. He didn't use notes. He communicated to transform rather than to simply inform. And His conclusions left His audiences breathless. In short, Jesus knew exactly who His audience was.

You may be wondering why I haven't mentioned anything about being dependent on God or anything about the Holy Spirit's help in the communication process. When I set out to write this book, I knew exactly who I was targeting—communicators of God's Word. And anyone who considers himself or herself to be a communicator of God's Word knows that without God we would not be able to do what we do. Without Him, we're nothing! To put it in television terms, the Holy Spirit is (or definitely should be) the executive producer behind every message. In television, the executive producer is like the CEO of a company. He or she is involved in every aspect of the program and has a say in everything, from the set design to the storyline to the selection of the cast. In short, he runs the show. He has the final say on every decision. And that's the way it should be with us when communicating God's Word. The Holy Spirit is to be the executive producer from the preparation of the message in the study to the communicated message on Sunday morning.

I heard a great story from David Jeremiah a few years ago that inspired a prayer I use every time I get up to speak. This is what he said:

> I read some time ago about a young minister from Scotland who got up in the pulpit to preach one day with the most

---

[160] Robinson, "Our Mission in a Changing World."

unbelievable self-confidence that you can imagine—proud and arrogant, puffed up, if you will. But when he got done preaching, it was evident to everybody, including himself, that the sermon he delivered was less than excellent. In fact, it was a flop. It was a failure. It was like a double dose of sleeping pills for the congregation. And when he came down from the pulpit that day, his head was down and he was feeling very bad. He was as defeated as he could be. And a dear elderly woman in the church, who had been there for years and had known God and walked with God, grabbed hold of the young man's arm, and she brought him over and she sat him down, and this is the advice she gave him: "Son, if you had gone up the way you came down, you would have come down the way you went up." I see you thinking that through. He went up in a spirit of arrogance and he came down in a sense of humility. And God wanted him to go up in a sense of humility, so that in the power of the Spirit he could have come down with a sense of confidence.[161]

What a fabulous story! Since the day I heard that, I never get up to speak without praying, "Lord, please have me go up the way You want me to go up, so I can come down the way You want me to come down." And to be quite honest, I don't know anyone who gets up to speak on Sunday morning who not only prays to God but, more importantly, is completely dependent on Him for the entire message. Every time Haddon Robinson gets up to speak, he prays, "Lord, get past me to the people, or get the people past me to You." Every weekend, Ed Young Jr. prays, "God, please use my voice box to communicate the words You want me to say today. Use me to creatively connect the life-changing message of Jesus Christ to every heart and every life here. And it's in His name that I pray. Amen."[162] And Rick Warren prays, "God, I love these people and they love me. I love You, and You love me and You love these people, and many of these people love You.

---

[161] David Jeremiah, "Love's Power Over Pride," POL 04, 1994.
[162] Young Jr., "Keys to Creative Communication," 13.

There is no fear in love. Perfect love casts out all fear. This is not an audience to be feared; this is a family to be loved. So love these people through me."[163] In short, it all comes down to what Bill Hybels once said: "Live in such vital union with Jesus Christ that His power and His might flow through your preaching. Pray like crazy; trust like crazy. Expect God to work and thank Him when He does."[164]

At the end of every television program, the first credit that rolls is the name of the program's executive producer. Likewise, when the credits roll at the end of a Sunday morning service, in our minds there should be only one name that appears under the words executive producer—God.

---

[163] Duduit, "Purpose-Driven Preaching," 16.
[164] Bill Hybels, "How to Improve Your Preaching," *Ruler of All*, Preaching Today, cassette no. 202.

Appendix

Answers to Exercise in Chapter 7

1. Don't leave home without it. **F**
2. Just do it. **G**
3. Melts in your mouth, not in your hands. **H**
4. Takes a licking and keeps on ticking. **B**
5. Reach out and touch someone. **I**
6. We bring good things to life. **A**
7. Good to the last drop. **C**
8. You're in good hands with **J**
9. Finger-lickin' good. **E**
10. How do you spell relief? **D**

A. General Electric
B. Timex
C. Maxwell House Coffee
D. Rolaids
E. Kentucky Fried Chicken
F. American Express
G. Nike
H. M & M Candies
I. AT&T
J. Allstate [Insurance]

BIBLIOGRAPHY

BOOKS

Byrne, Rhonda. *The Secret*. Hillsboro, OR: Beyond Words Publishing, 2006.

Craddock, Fred B. *As One Without Authority—Revised and with New Sermons*. St. Louis, MS: Chalice Press, 2001.

Duffet, Robert G. *A Relevant Word: Communicating the Gospel to Seekers*. Valley Forge, PA: Judson Press, 1995.

Gibson, Scott M., ed. *Making a Difference in Preaching: Haddon Robinson on Biblical Preaching*. Grand Rapids, MI: Baker Books, 1999.

Heath, Chip, and Dan Heath. *Made to Stick: Why Some Ideas Survive and Others Die*. New York, NY: Random House, 2007.

Henderson, David W. *Culture Shift: Communicating God's Truth to Our Changing World*. Grand Rapids, MI: Baker Books, 1998.

Litfin, Duane. *Public Speaking: A Handbook for Christians*. Grand Rapids, MI: Baker Books, 1992.

Miller, Calvin. *The Empowered Communicator: 7 Keys to Unlocking an Audience*. Nashville, TN: Broadman & Holman Publishers, 1994.

———. *Marketplace Preaching: How to Return the Sermon to Where it Belongs*. Grand Rapids, MI: Baker Books, 1995.

Robinson, Haddon. *Biblical Preaching: The Development and Delivery of Expository Messages*, 1st ed. Grand Rapids, MI: Baker Academic, 1980.

———. *Biblical Preaching: The Development and Delivery of Expository Messages*, 2nd ed. Grand Rapids, MI: Baker Academic, 2001.

Stanley, Andy, and Lane Jones. *Communicating for a Change*. Sisters, OR: Multnomah, 2006.

Weightman, Gavin. *Signor Marconi's Magic Box: The Most Remarkable Invention of the 19th Century and the Amateur Inventor Whose Genius Sparked a Revolution*. Cambridge, MA: Da Capo Press, 2003.

Willhite, Keith, and Scott M. Gibson (eds). *The Big Idea of Biblical Preaching—Connecting the Bible to People*. Grand Rapids, MI: Baker Books, 1998.

ARTICLES

Duduit, Michael, ed. "Creating Messages That Connect: An Interview with Alan Nelson." *Preaching* 20, no. 6 (May-June 2005): 16-24.

———, ed. "Expository Preaching in a Narrative World: An Interview with Haddon Robinson." *Preaching* 17, no. 1 (July-August 2001): 4-13.

———, ed. "Leading Through Preaching: An Interview with John Maxwell." *Preaching* 13, no. 4 (January-February 1998): 14-18.

———, ed. "A Preaching Interview with Bill Hybels." *Preaching* 7, no. 4 (January-February 1992): 2-10.

———, ed. "Preaching and the Holy Spirit: An Interview with Chuck Swindoll." *Preaching* 9, no. 3 (November-December 1993): 12-22.

———, ed. "Purpose-Driven Preaching: An Interview with Rick Warren." *Preaching* 17, no. 2 (September-October 2001): 6-17.

———, ed. "Understanding the Word: An Interview with Eugene Peterson." *Preaching* 23, no. 3 (November-December 2007): 22-27.

Mohler, Albert R. "Preaching to Joe Secular: An Interview with William E. Self." *Preaching* 4, no. 3 (November-December 1988): 3-6.

Sunukjian, Don. "Four Things That Can Happen When You Alliterate, and Four of Them Are Bad." *Preaching* 16, no. 3 (November-December 2000): 34-35.

Warren, Rick. "Preaching for Life Change: It's All in Learning to Preach Like Jesus." *Preaching* 19, no. 2 (September-October 2003): 9-19.

———. "Preaching to the Unchurched." *Preaching* 12, no. 2 (September-October 1996): 4-11.

Willhite, Keith. "A Sneak Preview at the Point: Sermon Introductions that Aim at Application." *Preaching* 5, no. 6 (May-June 1990): 17-22.

Young, Ed Jr., ed. "Communicating with Creativity." *Preaching* 20, no. 6 (May-June 2005): 8-13.

———. "Keys to Creative Communication." *Preaching* 21, no. 6 (May-June 2006): 12-20.

WEB SITES

Bellis, Mary. "Inventors: Philo Farnsworth." http://www.inventors.about.com/library/inventors/blfarnsworth.htm, accessed 24 Sept. 2005.

Garrett, Thomas A. "Casino Gambling in America and Its Economic Impacts." http://www.stlouisfed.org/community/assets/pdf/casinogambling.pdf, accessed 11 Feb. 2006.

Gimbel, Norman and Charles Fox. "Happy Days." http://www.cfhf.net/lyrics/happy.htm, accessed 11 Feb. 2006.

The World Fact Book: Field Listing—Radio Broadcast Stations. https://www.odci.gov/cia/publications/factbook/fields/2013.html, accessed 13 Dec. 2007.

Television Bureau of Advertising. www.tvb.org, accessed 25 Aug. 2009.

Unpublished Materials

Biography of the Millennium. Harry Smith (host and narrator). A&E, 1999.

Ganis, Sid. *78th Academy Awards.* ABC, 5 Mar. 2006.

Hybels, Bill. "How to Improve Your Preaching." *Ruler of All,* Preaching Today, cassette no. 202. Carol Stream, IL.

Jacks, Robert. "Preaching for the Ear." *True Holiness,* Preaching Today, cassette no. 190. Carol Stream, IL.

Jeremiah, David. "Love's Power Over Pride." Cassette no. POL 04, 1994.

Litfin, Duane. "A Preaching Style for this Generation." *Looking to Jesus,* Preaching Today, cassette no. 178. Carol Stream, IL.

Robinson, Haddon. "Biblical Preaching Lecture Series." Tyndale Seminary, 1984.

———. "Don't Just Do Something, Sit There." *The Empowered Communicator,* Preaching Today, cassette no. 138. Carol Stream, IL.

———. "How to Bring Clarity to Sermons." *Seeking Unity,* Preaching Today, cassette no. 189. Carol Stream, IL.

———. "How Can I Speak So An Audience Will Listen?" Tyndale Seminary, 13 June 2000.

———. "Our Mission in a Changing World." Denver Seminary, 4 Jan. 1991.

———. Personal Interview. 2 Sept. 2005.

———. "Preaching in a Television Age." *TV and Story,* Preaching Today, cassette no. 145. Carol Stream, IL.

———. "Speaking from a Listener's Point of View." Gordon-Conwell Theological Seminary. Ockenga Preaching Series, South Hamilton, MA, 1991.

Robinson, Haddon, Scott Gibson, and Jeffrey Arthurs. Discussion: "Doing Introductions." *PulpitTalk CD*, vol. 1, no. 2, Winter 2003.

———. "The Big Idea of the Sermon." *PulpitTalk CD*, vol. 4, no. 3, Spring 2006.

Robinson, Torrey. Personal Interview. 26 Sept. 2005.

Stanley, Andy. Personal Interview. 2 Aug. 2005.

———. "Trusting Christ at All Cost." 1993.

———. "When Things Seem Uncertain." Ocean Grove Rally, 22 June 2002.

Stowell, Joseph. "Followership." *Looking to Jesus*, Preaching Today, cassette no. 178. Carol Stream, Illinois.

Sunukjian, Don. Personal Interview. 10 July 2006.

Warren, Rick. "How to Communicate to Change Lives—Part 1." Preaching Today, cassette no. 120. Carol Stream, IL.

———. "How to Communicate to Change Lives—Part 2." Preaching Today, cassette no. 121. Carol Stream, IL.

CASTLE QUAY BOOKS

OTHER CASTLE QUAY TITLES INCLUDE:
Walking Towards Hope
The Chicago Healer
Seven Angels for Seven Days
Making Your Dreams Your Destiny
The Way They Should Go
The Defilers
The Cardboard Shack Beneath the Bridge
Keep On Standing
To My Family
Through Fire & Sea
One Smooth Stone
Vision that Works - **NEW!**
The Beautiful Disappointment - **NEW!**
Bent Hope - **NEW!**
Red Letter Christian - **NEW!**
The Leadership Edge - **NEW!**

BAYRIDGE BOOKS TITLES:
Counterfeit Code: Answering The Da Vinci Code
Heresies
Wars Are Never Enough: The Joao Matwawana Story
More Faithful Than We Think
Save My Children - **NEW!**
What the Preacher Forgot to Tell Me - **NEW!**
To Be Continued: The Story of the Salvation Army
in Woodstock - **NEW!**

For more information and to explore the rest
of our titles visit:
www.castlequaybooks.com